WOMEN

ARE

SCARY

So the thing about Melanie Dale is that she is really, genuinely funny. I didn't just smile when I read *Women Are Scary: The Totally Awkward Adventure of Finding Mom Friends* — I giggled. Chortled. *Guffawed*, even. But the other thing about Melanie Dale — and this is the part that gives her book so much substance — is that she is really, genuinely insightful. And while I wish this book had been around about ten years ago when I was in the throes of wondering why it sometimes seemed so difficult to connect with other mamas, I'm thrilled that Melanie's book is right here, right now. It's a fresh reminder that we're not meant to walk through motherhood alone, and it made me more grateful than ever for my mama friends who were strangers to me a decade ago — but have long since taken up residence in the deepest part of my heart. I'm so thankful for Melanie's humor, vulnerability, and honesty; women are going to be so encouraged by her words!

> SOPHIE HUDSON, author of *A Little Salty to Cut the Sweet* and blogger at BooMama.net

Women Are Scary has given me the great gift of knowing I am normal. Or at least semi-normal. Melanie Dale, with her funny, engaging words, perfectly captures the angst and joy and awkward moments that come our way as we try to navigate the world of finding our friends amongst a sea of minivans and soccer games. She will make you laugh out loud as you recognize pieces of yourself and, if you're like me, you'll find yourself nodding along until the last page when you close the book and breathe a deep sigh of relief that you're not alone.

> MELANIE SHANKLE, *New York Times* bestselling author of *Sparkly Green Earrings*

Melanie Dale, you are hilarious! Thank you for writing a book that not only made me laugh, but also inspired and encouraged me in my "momlationships"! Rock on, sister.

> REBECCA ST. JAMES, singer, author, and new mom

No one can make us quite as unsure about ourselves as another woman. And nothing can wound as much as the words that sometimes come from a friend. That's why you need this book. Because if you've been burned by women and friendship you need the reminder that it's worth it. Friendship is like oxygen for the soul and this is the handbook on how to overcome awkward and fall in love with friendship all over again.

> LISA-JO BAKER, author of *Surprised by Motherhood: Everything I Never Expected About Being a Mom* and community manager for incourage.me

Women are Scary is laugh out loud funny. But it's so much more than that. It's an honest exploration of the one thing so many moms fear — one another. And it's an invitation to know and be known in this thing we call motherhood.

Melanie is the real deal. Her humor, courage, and candor will inspire moms to "spur one another on" because, as Melanie writes, we aren't "just moms," we are world changers, and we are better, so much better, when we are with and for each other.

JEANNIE CUNNION, author of *Parenting the Wholehearted Child*

In *Women Are Scary,* Melanie dares to put candid words to the thoughts we've all secretly had about the ups and downs of motherhood. With both snort-out-loud humor and refreshing honesty, she encourages us to speak the truth as well — to ourselves and to each other as we develop new momlationships.

JAMIE C. MARTIN, blogger at SimpleHomeschool.net and SteadyMom.com and author of *Mindset for Moms*

Are you lonely too? With disarming honesty and humor, Melanie walks you through specific steps to find that "mommy girlfriend" you desperately need. Buy this book for every young mom you know. You will be giving her more than a book — you are giving her a guide to rich friendships.

SUSAN ALEXANDER YATES, speaker and bestselling author of many books including *And Then I Had Kids, Encouragement for Mothers of Young Children*

I found a kindred spirit in the pages of Melanie Dale's *Women are Scary.* She's clever and funny and makes me feel more normal in all of the things that I'm certain probably make me weird. She reminds us that making new friends can be hard, feel scary, but is also one of the most rewarding steps onto a limb we'll ever take. I laughed and cried and laughed some more … and then felt thankful that God gives us community and friendship to walk along this crazy road we call life.

LOGAN WOLFRAM, CEO Allume Ministries, author of *Curious Faith* (releasing 2016 with David C. Cook)

WOMEN ARE SCARY

THE TOTALLY AWKWARD ADVENTURE
OF FINDING MOM FRIENDS

melanie dale

ZONDERVAN®

ZONDERVAN

Women Are Scary
Copyright © 2015 by Melanie Dale

This title is also available as a Zondervan ebook. Visit www.zondervan.com/ebooks.

Requests for information should be addressed to:
Zondervan, 3900 Sparks Dr. SE, Grand Rapids, Michigan 49546

ISBN 978-0-310-34105-5

All Scripture quotations, unless otherwise indicated, are taken from The Holy Bible, *New International Version®, NIV®*. Copyright © 1973, 1978, 1984, 2011 by Biblica, Inc.® Used by permission. All rights reserved worldwide.

In order to protect the poor moms who are stuck on fourth base with me, I have changed their names to companions from *Doctor Who:* Rose, Martha, Donna, Amy, Rory, River, and Clara. I don't want to out them publicly and end up back on first, and my love for them transcends time and regenerations.

Cover design: James Hall
Interior illustration: Alex Dale and Greg Johnson
Interior design: Kait Lamphere

First printing January 2015 / Printed in the United States of America

To my fourth-basers. You know who you are.
And to Alex, who makes me brave.

CONTENTS

1. A Complete Lobotomy of the Heart 9
2. Women Are Scary 14
3. The Bases of Momlationships 20

Part 1
FIRST BASE

4. Mom-Date Virgin 27
5. Trolling for Moms 31
6. Small Talk for Small-Talk Haters 37
7. Mom Monsters 46
8. A Totally Judgmental Zit 53

Part 2
SECOND BASE

9. Dating on the Space-Time Continuum 65
10. The Group Date 72
11. Moms Can Change the World 77
12. How Not to Choke on Your Own Foot 84
13. Wield Your Weirdness Like a Boss 90
14. One Sock Short of a Pair 98
15. Overly Intense Eye Contact 102

Part 3
THIRD BASE

16. It's About to Get Real 109
17. The Superpower of Initiating 112
18. Navigating Your Child's Social Awkwardness 118
19. Dating (When You're) a "Working Mom" 126
20. The Anatomy of a Full-Frontal Hug 133

Part 4
FOURTH BASE

21.	Fourth-Basers, the Ultimate Friends	143
22.	Cranking Out a Mom Date If It Kills You	152
23.	Praying for a Bromance	160
24.	Rekindling the Momlationship	164
25.	Going Long Distance	171

Part 5
(NOT QUITE) HOME FREE

26.	Breaking Up Is Hard to Do: The Phaseout	179
27.	Breaking Up Is Hard to Do: The Confrontation	186
28.	When You Want to Mow Her Down with Your Minivan	197
29.	How to Get Your Mojo Back	205
30.	Screw Your Courage	213
31.	The Mother Network	220
32.	What the World Needs Now	224
Acknowledgments		231
Resources for Moms		233

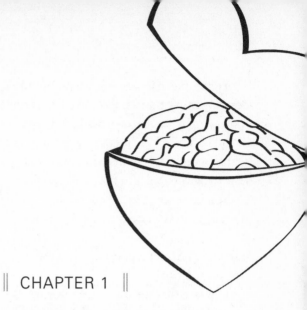

CHAPTER 1

A Complete Lobotomy
of the Heart

Principal: "At no point in your rambling, incoherent response was there anything that could even be considered a rational thought. Everyone in this room is now dumber for having listened to it. I award you no points, and may God have mercy on your soul." From *Billy Madison*[1]

I'm going to need a hug before I get started. I'm about to tell you about my relationships with women, but I'm not completely all that terrific at small talk, so can we skip ahead together and pretend like we've known each other for a while? Come over here and hug it out.

Okay. Thanks for that.

When we finally brought our Elliott home from neonatal intensive care and my husband had the gall to go back to work and leave me alone with our four-pound floppy baby, I felt overwhelmed.

I'm not the only one, right?

Young mothers are shriveling up into crusty dried raisins of despair. Every minute feels like forever when your two-year-old wants to put on her own socks and your five-year-old won't get in the bathtub. When you're a mom, you spend hours and hours sitting with other moms while your kids kick a soccer ball, learn how to blow bubbles in the pool, and shake maracas at music class.

You bat eyes at each other and glance away. It's awkward and someone always needs a diaper change and no one ever knows what to say. And most of us are frazzled and lonely, isolated in our minivans, schlepping bags, strollers, and munchkins to and fro across town.

I believe that we are better together. We make each other better moms, better humans. We need each other, because mothering is just too darn hard. *Women Are Scary* is our journey to each other, to finding our people and being other people's people, to learning how to bless each other and not destroy each other.

> I believe that we are better together. We make each other better moms, better humans.

My Lumpy, Bumpy Road

I'm the least likely person to write a book about motherhood. For years, I didn't want to be a mom. My boyfriend and I almost broke up because of it.

I have the most amazing parents in the universe. Ever. My mother stayed at home with my brother and me, and she could do it all. Baked goods greeted us when we came home from school. She was room mom, made homemade dinners every night, and we always had folded, clean clothes. When I was wracked out in pain every month because, unbeknownst to me, endometriosis was killing my fertility, she held my hand, brought me meds, and whispered to me to think of my toes. *Think of your toes, sweetie. Relax your toes.*

My mom gave everything she had to be a superhero to us, and

even so, we treated her like crap. Despite her self-sacrifice and outpouring of unconditional love, we took her for granted, took advantage of her, took her cookies and ran.

I told my boyfriend that I couldn't handle the sacrifice. I told him, "I'll have kids if I can be the dad. I don't want to be the mom." I could never live up to my mom, and my kids deserved nothing less. So I just wouldn't have them.

> "I'll have kids if I can be the dad.
> I don't want to be the mom."

We almost ended it there, but we were in love and total idiots. We decided to table the discussion and keep swing dancing and watching *Fletch* together. A few years later, we got married, and a few years after that, I felt the oddest urge to do the mom thing, like maybe the baby wouldn't start rejecting me right when it came out. Like maybe the first few years might be worth it. Like maybe even if I wasn't as good a mom as my mom, maybe I could be good enough. I found myself experiencing a complete lobotomy of the heart. I wanted a baby. I really, really wanted to be a mom.

Then I discovered I couldn't.

Every year that crept by felt like twelve deaths. I rode a monthly merry-go-round of up-up-up hope, hanging at the top, feeling *maybe this time*, then down-down-down into despair. Every month it felt like my dream baby died. On the road of infertility, I discovered how far I was willing to go for my child. I would endure any needle, any surgery, anything for my baby.

And finally after five years, I held him. The little preemie red raisin who survived my body, barely, and lay in his incubator hooked up to all the beeping things. He made me a mommy. And I loved him.

I loved being Mommy. I loved it so much that I tried to make more babies—more needles and science and more brokenness.

My body told me, "You're done," and after months of counseling, I began to feel whole again. God glued me back together, shard by broken shard, and then surprised me with an unexpected gift, a passion for adoption—*passion*, not fallback. Adoption became the deep desire of my heart, not a backup plan.

We worked and waited for our daughter for two years, and it still surprises me how hard I work for the children I didn't used to want.

We brought our daughter home from Ethiopia when she was almost two. Now she's four, our incubator boy is six, and as I finish this book, I'm sitting in a cozy apartment in Latvia with the nine-year-old girl who has captivated us all. Three continents, three kids, and three unique journeys to each of them.

Powerhouse Women

As I've met moms, from the ones at our local playground to the ones advocating for orphans around the world, I'm flabbergasted that I ever had a dim view of motherhood. I saw it as giving something up. It never occurred to me what I'd gain. My rough road to motherhood grew my character and readied me to join this incredible group of women, powerhouse women changing lives around the world together.

> I saw motherhood as giving something up.
> It never occurred to me what I'd gain.
> ===================

Mothers are strong and powerful, and when we join together in relationship, mountains move. The girl who once turned up her nose at motherhood fought tooth and nail to enter in. I'm still fighting for my kids.

As I gained kids, I gained so much more. I entered into a living, loving organism of motherhood. Society fears our power, seeks to divide us on issues, but when we pull together for the common good of generations, we change the world.

So I'm here, oddly enough, the girl who didn't want to be a mom, the girl who couldn't be a mom, trying to break down these crazy things I call momlationships. You know, those relationships that come with car pools and cupcakes, friendships borne at T-ball games and in quiet corners feeding babies.

Whether you became a mom accidentally or on purpose, hesitantly or with gusto, you're here now, and sooner or later, we're going to meet at a park or soccer game or ballet class. And it might get awkward.

In this space of a book I invite us to come together. So much of mothering doesn't seem to apply to me—like Pinterest. And other parts of me don't seem to apply to mothering—like my unabashed movie quoting. If these pages don't apply to you, read my story and have the freedom and grace to live your own. No matter who you are, you are welcome.

Notes

1. *Billy Madison*, directed by Tamra Davis, Universal Pictures, 1995.

‖ CHAPTER 2 ‖

Women Are Scary

The Doctor: "There're a lot of things you need to get across this universe. Warp drive ... wormhole refractors ... You know the thing you need most of all? You need a hand to hold." From *Doctor Who*[1]

I was sitting in a roomful of women I barely knew, watching a video in which Bible teacher Beth Moore got down in someone's face and declared, "I love women!"[2]

Ooh, I thought to myself, *I don't think I love women*. Women are scary, complicated creatures.

The very next moment, something inside me bubbled up and I prayed inside my head, "God, help me to love women."

Nothing happened. I didn't feel the earth shake or my insides quiver. I finished watching the video, picked up my daughter in the nursery, and moved on with my life.

Never did I suspect that God would answer that little prayer in such a big way. I've spent the last four years blogging about orphan care and our adoption journeys. As a sponsorship coordinator for Children's HopeChest, I've traveled to Uganda several times where we partner with a group of widows in a small village to serve about three hundred orphans and vulnerable children. Loving the women in Uganda came naturally to me. Loving the women right here at home felt harder.

Looking back over the last couple of years, since praying that prayer, I've realized that God has completely rewired my heart. I find myself asking questions, listening to the hearts and hurts of the women around me, and offering bear hugs with abandonment. Where I wanted to run, I now leap to encourage. Where I felt defensive, I now celebrate our differences.

> Where I wanted to run, I now leap to encourage. Where I felt defensive, I now celebrate our differences.

In the 'burbs where I do life, we live in an independent, isolated culture. As I've traveled to Uganda and witnessed material poverty in the village with which we're partnered, I've discovered that my culture struggles with a different kind of poverty. We don't lack food, clean water, or clothing, but we lack relationships. Whereas my friends in northern Uganda reside in small mud homes and live life together, outside, as a community, gathering at the borehole for water, working their gardens side by side, and looking out for each other's children, we live in elaborate homes with multiple rooms and water that comes out of our own faucets. We drive our cars into garages and close the doors behind us, and we can go days and weeks without interacting with the neighbors unless we're intentional about making friends.

And while I will continue to champion the orphans and widows whom I love, I've realized that it's no less noble to reach out to the hurting moms and kids right in my own community. If we can learn how to develop real, soul-soothing relationships, there's no stopping what we can do together for our kids, our families, and the world. But first we have to stop being scary and scared of each other.

Hiding from Women

I meet so many women who say they had few girlfriends growing up. They preferred to hang out with guys, because guys were less complicated and more fun. That was me. And apparently there were a lot of us who felt that way. Many girls were difficult and hurtful, and we just gave up, took our toys, and went home. We hid. Some of us are still hiding.

> Many girls were difficult and hurtful, and we just
> gave up, took our toys, and went home.

A "friend" in high school once said of me, "I've spent a year trying to get to know the real Melanie, and I've decided there's just not that much to get to know." Twenty years later, I still remember that. And someone else is probably still remembering something mean that I can't take back.

Words hurt, and they are the weapons of choice for a lot of us women. We build relationships and hang out with other women and think we're connected, only to have mean girls shatter us with clever words. Maybe you've been on the receiving end of a word bullet, or maybe you've been the shooter.

We leave high school, but if we aren't careful, we never leave high school. We just grow up, acquire kids, and have even more things about which to bicker. From how you feed your baby to how you educate your first grader, we argue and scare the crap out of each other. Other women can be scary! We all have big opinions, and you never know what's going to set us off. *Why bother. It's too awkward and complicated. Who has time for other women?* Right? I've thought it.

My First Real Girlfriend

In college, they force you to have roommates. And for many of us, that was hard too. Here were people from whom you couldn't get away. You just shared a space and hurt and annoyed each other month after month. By the end of my sophomore year, I was ready to move into a single room and give up on girls altogether. I felt unlovable. Argumentative. Misunderstood.

I'll never forget casually mentioning that I was thinking about moving into a single room for junior year and one of my roommates saying something like, "I'll go wherever, as long as we're together." Maybe she didn't say it that way. But in my head, people started soft-shoe dancing and there were cartoon birdies. Another girl actually wanted to keep being my friend, to keep living with me. I couldn't believe it.

She was my roommate for two more years. We were in each other's weddings. You could not pick two more different people. As a quiet person, she taught me to listen. Well, at least I got better at it. When I was a crazy psycho because my boyfriend took his darn ol' time proposing, she gave me grace. She introduced me to the pomegranate, and we listened to Big Bad Voodoo Daddy together. We weren't moms yet. But she was my first real day-in, day-out, doing-life-together relationship.

We attended our first women's retreat together, hosted by the women at our church. At that point I was still learning how to be a little bit normal, how to navigate female relationships. My life as a theatre major, a fairly untalented one, consisted of daily rehearsals in which I stood in the back and played the silent role of wench or maid and practiced carrying trays and not drawing attention to myself while wearing a corset and petticoat.

On the night of my first women's retreat, I of course had wench or maid rehearsal in my whalebones and came to the retreat late, tired, and my insides just a little squeezed. My boobs were relieved to be out of the corset and away from my throat, and I guess I was exploring my diaphragmatic freedom, because before I knew what I was doing, I burped loudly in front of everyone.

I liked burping. Burping was awesome. And then an entire room filled with older church ladies turned to stare at me and I could tell they were mustering the good Christian grace for which they'd trained, and I realized that maybe my parents weren't the only ones who thought burping in public was a bad idea. Having girlfriends and being a lady might require sacrifice on my part. No more burping wench-maid. I wasn't sure what I thought about this.

I Don't Quite Fit

Years later, I still love Jesus, and burping, and sometimes in spite of myself and my complete weirdness, I still go to these things called women's conferences. They're filled with lovely ladies and prayer and I'm always just a little on edge, like I don't quite fit and if they only knew what was going on inside of me ... you know, besides gas. In a room full of Christian women I always secretly panic that I'm going to somehow lose control and scream the f-bomb over and over until they drag me out by my Bible.

> In a room full of Christian women I always secretly panic that I'm going to somehow lose control and scream the f-bomb over and over until they drag me out by my Bible.
> ===

And sometimes when I'm hanging out with friends I worry in my head that I'll bust out my bilingual Christianese and start talking in church words, and they'll bless my butt out of Dodge and spank my exegesis.

And that right there illustrates how remarkably bizarre I am, if I'm worried that I'm too Christianese *and* that I'm a total wreck and too morally repugnant. If someone this screwed up in the brain can make friends, then you can, too. I'm sure of it. And if you read this book and still crash and burn, well, then, at least you'll have someone to blame. (*Disclaimer: Reading this book will not automatically give you friends. I have no formal training in people or relationships and am in no way an expert on friendships. Also, sometimes I'm serious and sometimes I'm kidding, and I leave it to your discernment to figure out when. If you experience relational upheaval after reading this book, it's not my fault, although I'd be happy to give you a full-frontal hug if that'll make you feel better.)

When you get past the scariness, other moms are fun. You'll find that they're covered in vomit just like you. They try not to go off on their kids just like you. They try to find time and energy for sex just like you. They crave adult conversation with someone else who understands, just like you.

Women Are Scary is an invitation to momlationships. Girls are tricky and weird. We're too opinionated and insecure. We tear each other apart. And we need each other.

I witnessed the perfect illustration of female relationships as I waited for my kids in the pickup line at preschool. I watched as two three-year-old girls held hands and tried to walk in opposite directions. They yanked and yanked each other back and forth. They were very angry. They were bossy. They tried and tried to get the other one to go their way. Because their way was better. They knew. No matter how hard they yanked and yanked, they each had their own idea about the right way to do things. But in all the yanking and bossing, they never let go. They held hands tighter and tighter.

That's a relationship with a girl. We hold hands. We don't let go. Because we need each other. We yank and yank, but we don't let go.

So this is a call to find your girls, grab hands, and don't let go. We are better together. Put on your best sweatpants and let's get started.

Notes

1. "The Almost People," *Doctor Who*, British Broadcasting Corporation, May 28, 2011.

2. Beth Moore, "James: Mercy Triumphs," Lifeway Christian Resources, 2011, DVD.

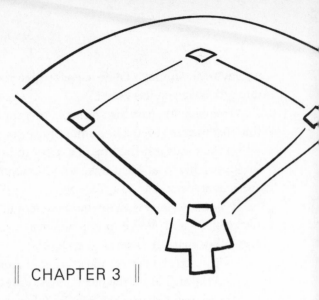

CHAPTER 3

The Bases of Momlationships

Barbossa: "The code is more what you'd call 'guidelines' than actual rules."

From *Pirates of the Caribbean*[1]

You get married. You conjure up some kids. You've kissed dating good-bye.

Or have you?

When you show up at the park for the first time with your little ones spilling out of the van (along with a healthy amount of cups and dirty napkins, if you're like me), scan the swing sets for anyone you might recognize, and notice that all the other moms are already hanging out in pairs, you realize that your dating years have only just begun.

When you were dating your man, you ate dinners for which you didn't pay and walked through doors that he opened for you. When you date other moms, you pack extra baggies of healthy snacks and push doors open with your face while schlepping car seats. When you were dating your man, you wore incredible outfits and said, "Oh, this old thing? I just threw it on last minute." When you date other moms, you wear tees and yoga pants and say, "Oh, this old thing? My toddler just threw up on it."

I recently met a new friend and I was thinking about our budding momlationship. Our kids attend some of the same activities, and we've enjoyed chatting while they harass their various coaches. I really like her, and I think she likes me too. And just like the other kind of dating, there are bases.

Just like the other kind of dating, there are bases.
====================

First Base

First base is hanging out while your kids are in activities together. You make encouraging comments about each other's kids as they scream hysterically and hit each other with kick boards and pretend light sabers. I like to go ahead and act a little weird on first base, just to give them a taste for where they're headed if they stick with me. I'm terrible at small talk, so if I survive this phase with another mom, then I know she's either desperate for a friend or really into me. I go too deep too soon, which scares off a mom just asking how many kids I have. "Do you mean in my home, or in orphanages around the world? Here locally, or in a village in Uganda? Have you ever considered sponsoring a child? Wait, where are you going? Wanna hear about malaria and deworming?"

Second Base

Second base is a park playdate outside of scheduled activities. At this point, you're hanging out because you want to and you set it up ahead of time. Your kids like each other. You like each other. This could be the start of something beautiful. At the park, you're still on neutral territory. I usually throw in a snort laugh right around here. The conversation could wade into deeper waters. Someone might toss out an opinion or two. Keep it loving, girls. Keep it gracious. If you love gluten-free, feel free to talk about it. If you love Jesus, feel free to talk about him. Just don't start talking in absolutes, making broad, generalizing statements, because you may never make it to third.

We do that sometimes, don't we?

And overly intense eye contact, never use this while discussing homeschooling, gluten, gun control, breastfeeding, marriage, red dye number 40, infertility, or Jesus. I may have left out a few things. If there's a subject that might cause you to stop blinking and/or breathing, save it for fourth base and don't unleash it at the park.

Third Base

Third base is a playdate at one of your houses. This is a tricky base because your kids are now on home court and your new friend is going to see your daughter body-slam her toddler to the ground and take back the toy that he just picked up. She will see the layer of dried-on grime coating your kid's chair at the table, and she will notice the unflushed dooky from your son's morning dump. Third base is not for the weak. It's about to get real in here. There could be laundry piles. You better have the relational stamina for this kind of commitment.

By third base, I'm full-frontal hugging, so prepare for that. If you're my third-base friend, get ready for our boobs smashed up together while I ask how you're doing right in your ear. If you answer that with any kind of trauma, I'm a-gonna pull it right back together for another mash-up, breathe some words of encouragement into your ear, then pull back for some heavy eye contact. (Upon reading this, my husband informed me, "Who are you kidding? You're easy. You go for full-frontal hugging on first base." So I'm a hug-slut. Bring it in, ladies. I'm ready.)

Fourth Base

Fourth base is hanging out without the kids. I know. Whoa. The kids have become optional. You can actually meet at a restaurant, movie theater, coffee shop, or bookstore and talk. Uninterrupted. For hours. Just because you want to, not because you're killing time while your kids do their thing. You have arrived. This person is worth spraying on your fancy jeans. Feel free to bust out your full-blown honk laugh, talk about how soy gives you diarrhea, and how you worry that you're a crappy mom. You've found your person. She loves you for you.

To my fourth-basers: I love you more than words can say. Let's get our date on soon. I'll dust off my fancy jeans, and we can eat Thai coconut soup and talk about not our kids. We're gonna get hot and heavy, mom-style. Fourth base for moms is so much better than dating fourth base. There's dessert, staying out till the security guard kicks you out of the mall parking lot, and no walk of shame as you crawl into bed next to your racked-out hubs. One fourth-base mom date will last me for a couple of months. It's just that fulfilling.

Jump in, girls. Dating for moms is super fun, and you just might get lucky.

Notes

1. *Pirates of the Caribbean*, directed by Gore Verbinski, Walt Disney Pictures, 2003.

Part 1

FIRST BASE

‖ CHAPTER 4 ‖

Mom-Date Virgin

Woman: "I'll have what she's having."

From *When Harry Met Sally*[1]

I remember my first mom date. I was a mom-date virgin, and my own mom set me up. Yep, the girl writing about mom dating had to have her mommy help her find friends. We were new to parenting, new to town, and living over my parents' garage while we looked for a house. My mom's close friend also had a daughter who was moving here, and they swore adamantly that we'd click. She told me exuberantly, "I found your new best friend!" I had my doubts.

The first time I met her was at a little first-base *Hello My Name Is* in the lobby after church. I was recently C-sectioned and lumpy, unaccustomed to the Georgia summer heat and covered in sweat and my own breast milk. My clothes were packed and nothing fit and I'd borrowed my mom's shirt that morning. I felt like an armpit, like my entire person was one big armpit with eyes.

> I felt like an armpit, like my entire person
> was one big armpit with eyes.
> ═══════════

Across the church lobby, this tanned priestess named Rose strode toward me with her mile-long legs balancing perfectly on four-inch high heels. This was during her experiment with veganism, so she looked incredible, like what's the lowest possible amount of body fat you can have without being dead? That. Her hair was long and shiny, and she balanced her toddler on her chiseled hip while her three-year-old stood nearby. She smiled and was the nicest person on the planet and I couldn't decide if I wanted to kill her with my thoughts or maybe ask her if she wanted to snuggle.

A few days later, Rose picked us up in her Cheerio-encrusted van and we went to lunch with our boys. I remember looking at the inside of her van with amazement. It was the most disgusting thing I'd ever seen, and me with my three-month-old baby couldn't fathom what could cause that level of grossness.

Via Twitter @UnexpectedMel

I love our van. It feels like another room in our house, a room that never, ever gets cleaned.

Oh. One million blown-out diapers and three billion baggies of cereal later, I understand. Six years later, I am proud to drive my own sticky Petri Dish of Love around town.

Elliott was three months old, and I remember the day because it was the first time he wore shoes. Rose and I secretly sneered at the thought of our mothers being able to set us up. I really never put much faith in my mother's ability to find me a friend, but she nailed it.

Rose was perfect. I thought she knew everything. We ran the bases together until that magical night when we went out without kids, and our friendship has lasted through babies, adoptions, and moving out of state. Since my maiden voyage into mom dating, I've forged delicious relationships with several other fourth-basers too. And I'll always have my Rose. She's my people, and she loves me even though she knows how gross I am.

Two Unexpected Mamas

Remembering this makes me think of another first mom date, involving a different kind of virgin. In the book of Luke, after the angel Gabriel informed Mary that God would make her pregnant, he didn't leave her to wrestle with the ramifications of that disclosure all by her lonesome. Right after telling her she was going to have God's baby, he shared that her relative Elizabeth was six months pregnant. Gabriel acted as a mom-dating matchmaker, getting these two unlikely miracle mamas together for some God-ordained support.

Mary hurried to Elizabeth's house in the hill country, and as she greeted Elizabeth, the Bible says this is what happened:

> When Elizabeth heard Mary's greeting, the baby leaped in
> her womb, and Elizabeth was filled with the Holy Spirit. In
> a loud voice she exclaimed: "Blessed are you among women,
> and blessed is the child you will bear! But why am I so favored,
> that the mother of my Lord should come to me? As soon as the
> sound of your greeting reached my ears, the baby in my womb
> leaped for joy. Blessed is she who has believed that the Lord
> would fulfill his promises to her!"   LUKE 1:41–45

The first playdate of the New Testament commenced, and these girls walked through pregnancy together for three months. If that isn't a home run of a mom date, I don't know what is.

These two unexpected mamas found each other. Mary was a teenage virgin knocked up by the Holy Spirit getting the stink eye from society and Elizabeth was an infertile old woman finding herself pregnant when others her age were well into empty nesting. There was nothing "typical" about these girls, and they shared nothing in common with most of the other mothers around them.

Maybe your age or your job or your marriage, or lack thereof, puts you in the margins of "typical" motherhood. All of us come to motherhood by different paths and choose different methods. Some things we choose and some are chosen for us.

If you're on the edges, if you feel like you don't fit into the traditional view of motherhood or didn't come by it the traditional way, you are welcome here. I've always felt too infertile, too doing it the wrong way. From the decision to invite scientists into my womb to our pursuit of adoptions, I've experienced everything from ginger disdain to blatant reproof. If you feel like you're hanging onto the edge of motherhood and not so sure about the whole club, I'm with you, I'm for you, and you are sooo welcome here.

Notes

1. *When Harry Met Sally*, directed by Rob Reiner, MGM, 1989.

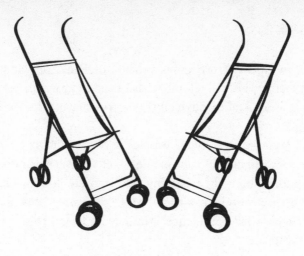

‖ CHAPTER 5 ‖

Trolling for Moms

Harriet Michaels: "What do you look for in a woman you date?"
Charlie Mackenzie: "Well, I know everyone always says sense of humor, but I'd really have to go with breast size."

From *So I Married an Axe Murderer*[1]

If you could pick your ideal friends, whom would you choose? Would they be exactly like you or really different?

I have a diverse group of friends, and I love having people from different backgrounds and with different passions and personalities around me. There are a few things that I look for in my closest friends, though. I'm drawn to those mamas who let me be me, who laugh at my jokes, who share deeply, and who are a little what I like to call scary-intense.

I want someone who's going to go ballistic over kids without food, stuck in orphanages, or held in slavery. I want someone who's going to get in my face if I'm out of line and hold up my arms when I'm tired of fighting for justice. I want someone who cackles and speaks truth and is either a total geek or glad I am. I want a mama who will tell me what I need to hear, not just what I want to hear. And through all that scary intensity, I want her to love me.

So for you, who are your people? If you're looking for moms with whom you can go running, let's get you out on trails chatting up girls about their jogging strollers. Do you love baking brownies? Let's find you a friend who loves eating brownies. Do you struggle with confidence? You need a friend who excels at encouragement.

Finding friends also means learning how to be a good friend, so we're also working on our own stuff too. As we seek to encourage and support the moms around us, we become exactly the kind of friend we want to have.

Where are you going to find your people? The library for story time, a "mommy and me" class, the preschool pickup line, a young moms' group at a church, or the sidelines at a soccer game. Moms are everywhere, and most of us are a little bit lonely and starved for adult conversation. If you work outside of the home, you may spend time with other adults professionally, but you still need other moms to talk to. Stay-at-home moms just need people to talk to, period.

Via Twitter @UnexpectedMel

Well I'm off to play dollhouse w/my 3yo, the game where time stops and I think I've been playing for an hour but really it's been 4 minutes.

My favorite relationships are the ones that start out bonding over our kids but transition to talking about books we're reading, our thoughts on different issues, or just straight up laughter about something absurd. I love coming together with other women over coffee to solve the world's problems while a few feet away, our children learn how to share. My girlfriends make me a better mom, a better friend, a better wife, just ... better.

I'd met Martha through another friend and really liked her. She was pregnant with her fourth child and looked like a supermodel.

No, seriously. Picture the hottest pregnant chick you've ever seen. She was always draped in something fabulous, and her third trimester looked better than my six months postpartum.

One day I was crying about my dog, and I needed a friend. I should mention that at this point Martha was a cat person. But something made me call her and invite myself over. She is gracious and kind and makes hospitality look effortless, so I rang her doorbell.

I quickly learned that even though she had four kids, Martha was a voracious reader who had delightful opinions about everything and was going to change the world. As I got to know her, the phrase "just a mom" catapulted out of my head never to return.

I drove back to her house again and again, and she helped me decorate my messy new place. We talked of books and writing and faith and events and ideas. She showed me that as a mom I can still take interest in other things besides my kids. Isn't that a relief.

We have different friends for different aspects of our personalities. I have my sci-fi-loving friends for movie watching. These are my "get my references" friends. And I have the friends I call when I'm cracking down the center and need someone to pray for my brain.

So, figure out who your people are, then start trolling.

The first time I met one of my favorite moms was at church. I was working in the three-year-old room and this mom would come pick up her daughter, and we'd say hi at those weekly interactions. Then at a mutual friend's party we got to talking and I really liked her. She was funny and outgoing, which meant I didn't have to talk as much — just the way I like it. One of the first things that stood out, though, was her obsession with our heights. I am 5'2 ½" on a good day. She's probably 5'1". She walked right up to me and asked me who I thought was taller while standing in her three inch wedges and craning her neck for length. I was standing in my flats and laughing because who says this to a stranger? I made her slide her cheating shoes off and we stood back-to-back while our husbands confirmed that I am indeed taller. And then she went into a diatribe about how she didn't feel like she looked shorter and we were probably really the same height and I couldn't possibly be that much taller. Now that I know her better, it cracks me up that she put so much thought into it and occasionally still makes me stand back-to-back with her to see if anything has changed. — *Kim T.*

Where to Look

You've just had a baby. Or you've moved to a new town. Perhaps you've been going it alone for a while and now you're looking to try out this mom dating thing. Whatever the reason, you're on the prowl for a friend. Where do you look?

Moving to a new state as a new mom felt daunting. Not only was I a new mom, but I was a new Southerner too. From burp cloths to sweet tea, everything was new. When my leaky boobs and I actually made it out of the house with my little projectile-spit-upping pumpkin, I didn't know where to look for friends, but I knew I needed some more, and my mommy couldn't help me with all of them.

Via Twitter @UnexpectedMel

Today I got everybody ready for the pool, headed that way, only to discover that I'd forgotten to put my bathing suit on under my cover-up.

I found myself stalking other moms in the drop-off line of the church nursery. Here was an entire line of mamas schlepping two-ton diaper bags, wiping rash cream off the hems of their skirts. While we bounced our whimpering babes up and down, I chatted them up about nap schedules and how the hour in the church service now felt like a date night with my husband.

We've just moved again, locally, and I find myself back in that place of introducing myself again and again to the other mamas around the neighborhood. This summer at the pool, feeling over-exposed in my swimsuit but determined to meet the neighbors, I walked from chair to chair, waving like a five-year-old and saying, "Hi! I'm Melanie. I'm new." Not the most creative pickup line but usually effective.

When you're a mom, the neighborhood bus stop feels like the new techno club, except without the cover of strobe lights and fog machines. It's completely intimidating to walk up to a group of moms and introduce yourself. I like to pick off the loners on the edges of groups first, then work my way in to meet everyone.

Music and art classes for small children are another surefire way to meet other people in the same stage of life, and it's an easy segue to invite them out for lunch after the class. I'm grateful to the moms who invited me for playdates when I was the newbie, and I try to pay it forward now when I meet new moms.

Just as I felt like my circle of friends was set, our family created another department in our lives . . . homeschooling. This past fall I began homeschooling my daughter. It has opened a whole new world of friendship possibilities. Everyone we have met through our homeschool group is so gracious and kind. The first day we met as a class I was drawn to a mom who was new to homeschooling like me. We were in the same boat and able to share stories and challenges about homeschool life! Turns out her son and my daughter sit next to each other in class and have become fast friends. As we juggle our new routine, pace ourselves to get schoolwork done, and still keep up with our old friends, I am reminded that making new friends is a slow and awkward process. — *Julie P.*

Don't be afraid to set people up. One friend invited me over with a few people and introduced me to someone who's now one of my closest friends. I'm not making this up; it was like, "Hey, you're infertile and just had a baby through in vitro. This is your new friend. She's infertile, too, and adopted a child. You're both crazy loudmouths with a ridiculous amount of passion about a number of subjects. Discuss your endometriosis and laparoscopies. Go." In a completely nonawkward way. And now she and I are fourth-basers. Badabing, badaboom.

If you experience an awkward crash and burn, don't panic. I have been there. My son doesn't quite understand boundaries with neighbors or pick up on social cues. One time we went for a walk and he found some "friends." He immediately ran up and started playing in their front yard, and since the parents were outside, I tried to strike up a conversation. As I asked question after question, received one-word replies, no questions back, and the other kids stood in their yard like *Children of the Corn* and stared at my son, I realized that either these people were not in the market for new friends or they'd just told their kids that Santa wasn't real. I sweetly called for Elliott as he was helping himself to the toys in their garage and he walked quizzically toward me. I backed away slowly, smiling and giving a courtesy wave. "Okay, well, soooo great to meet you guyzzz ..."

Small talk is hard, but it doesn't have to be 100 percent miserable, so we should probably talk about that now.

Notes

1. *So I Married an Axe Murderer*, directed by Tommy Schlamme, TriStar Pictures, 1993.

CHAPTER 6

Small Talk for
Small-Talk Haters

Inigo Montoya: "I do not mean to pry, but you don't by any chance happen to have six fingers on your right hand?"

Man in Black: "Do you always begin conversations this way?"

From *The Princess Bride*[1]

When you're trolling for moms, you practice pickup lines, but instead of "Heaven just lost an angel," you try "Your kids are so sweet," "I love your workout skort," or "Nice Moby wrap."

Have you ever tried to befriend another mom only to have it die an awkward little death? Just me? My kids were all born on different continents, so my strikeouts usually go something like this:

Me: Hi, I'm Melanie. I'm new here. Have you been coming here long?

Other Mom (OM): Oh, hi, I'm OM. Yeah, we've been doing this for a while *(indicates many other friends nearby)*.

Me: Oh, cool. Which kids are yours?

OM: Penelope over there. Who are your kids?

Me: Those three over there.

OM: Are they all three yours?

Me: Yep!

OM: I mean, are they all your own?

Me: Uh-huh. I own them all.

OM: I mean, are they your real kids?

Me: Yes. They are all real. No blow-up dolls in the bunch.

OM: The two oldest are yours and where's the youngest one from?

Me: Two of them are adopted and one was created in a lab.

OM: Um ...

Me: The oldest one, with hair identical to mine, is adopted from Latvia and our newest child, oldest and newest, haha. The middle child, with blond hair and blue eyes who looks nothing like me, is biologically related to me. The youngest one is adopted from Ethiopia.

OM: Ohhhhh. My brother-in-law went on a mission trip one time ... ohhhh ... I forget where ... Nicaragua.

Me: Okay, well, it was really nice to meet you!

And I'm a total geek, so sometimes this happens:

Me: Hi! I'm Melanie! I'm new!

OM: Hi, Melanie. I'm not new.

Me: What's your daughter's name?

OM: Buffy.

Me: The Vampire Slayer?! That's amazing! Ahhhh! I love that show! I have every episode on DVD. Most amazing writing EVER. Joss Whedon is completely brilliant. Oh! (*clap clap clap*) It's so great to meet another Whedonite!

OM: She's named after my husband's grandmother. I've never seen that show. Isn't it about demons?

Me: Um, yeah, pray for me?

OM: Okay, well, it was really nice to meet you!

Awkward small talk that fails to gain traction is enough to make you never want to leave the house. Or at least keep your nose buried in your smartphone while you wait for Baby Obiwan to finish up at Soccer Tots.

I'm one of those closet introverts posing as an extrovert. You know what I mean? When I tell people I'm an introvert, they spray spit on my face with the force of their exuberant guffaws. The girl snort-laugh jazz-handing in the middle of the crowded room is an introvert? Please.

Okay, so maybe I'm a borderline introvert. I love people oh so much, but I fill up in my little closet all by my lonesome — no talkie, just writey. On planes, I try not to make eye contact or so much as tap the elbow rest with my arm for fear I'll have to chat (unless the crossword in my airline magazine is already worked, and then I'm organizing a plane-wide search for a fresh one).

> **Via Twitter @UnexpectedMel**
>
> Okay people, we are wayyy too timely in the car pool pickup line for preschool. Can we all agree now that 10 minutes late is the new On Time?

The same is true for those first-base moments. When my kids are at practices, events, school functions, or birthday parties, I hunker down inside myself.

If I'm waiting for them, I bring my iPad and guzzle down whatever book I've been digesting. We mamas know how fast those waiting moments go. I see all of us reading our phones, Kindles, iPads, and actual books (ah, my love of actual books ...) during these precious minutes to ourselves.

Drop the iPad and Just Hang Out

Well, lately I've thought a lot about dating other moms and realize now just how many of us struggle with first base. So one day while my kids were in their swimming lessons, I left my iPad in my upcycled flour sack/purse and hung out with the other moms in the room.

I'm not going to lie. A few moments of silence made me ogle my dormant tablet, but I just sat, and then this beautiful thing happened. We started talking, sharing kids' names and our names. We rooted for each other's kids in the pool. We talked lack-of-nap times, food allergy issues, and girls versus boys when it comes to attitude shenanigans.

First-base stuff. Nothing world changing. Or is it?

> When mamas who shape the future start sharing
> and laughing … isn't that world changing?

———————

When mamas who shape the future start sharing and laughing … isn't that world changing? When the daily stress of the schedules and tantrums and budgets slides off our shoulders and onto the pool-water-soaked floor, that changes our world. Sharing experiences from our unique perspectives creates camaraderie in our overlapping lives. We make music in the rhythm of motherhood.

On first base. This is where it starts. This is where we gather the strength and resolve to laugh off our heavy burdens and agree to do it again tomorrow.

Maybe small talk isn't really small.

We need each other so much. Motherhood is meant to be shared. I'm sure of it.

I will continue to carry around my beloved iPad. (*Disclaimer: No iPads were harmed in the writing of this book. My tablet with its happy pink cover is smiling supportively at me on my desk. Long live technology.) But I am falling head over heels in deep, deep love with the mamas in my life, these precious girls who know more than I do about so much.

We share so many of the same pressures, insecurities, and frustrations, and doing just that, *sharing them*, somehow diffuses the power these worries have over us. There's fellowship in frustration. When one mom is upset with her button-pushing toddler, I know that frazzled feeling. And it's such a relief when we find out we're not alone. We're not alone! When we lower our guard, reach out, and say, "I've been there," we acknowledge and kindle the sisterhood of motherhood. (See what I did there? Kinnndlllle.)

Have you ever met someone who loves small talk? I meet so many people who hate small talk. I hate small talk. Small talk is boring and awkward. I don't think anybody really likes it, but we have to soldier through to get to the protein-packed tempeh of the relationship.

First base is where we lift our eyes off our own mess long enough to smile at the mama across from us. First base is small talk and encouragement and finding common ground. It's discovering we're on Team Mom together. And if we're on the same team, then that makes us teammates.

The Mama Booty Pat

Athletes have the little booty pat that we see happening on the sidelines. It conveys "You're doing a great job," "We're on the same team," and "Go get 'em, tiger."

We need a booty pat for mommies.[2] What can I do when I see you at Target and your daughter is waving her sass around and I can tell you're frustrated but you're handling it like a champ? Booty pat.

Okay, but not—because even I think that's crossing a line. Maybe I'll just settle for telling you.

Hey, mama. You're doing a great job. I got my own crazy going on in my cart right here. We had a meltdown in the Chapstick aisle the likes of which this store, this entire franchise, has never seen. But we're holding the line, soldiering on, and we're doing good work.

Moms need to hear that we're doing a good job. We don't get performance reviews for motherhood. We hear all kinds of judgment from everyone, from our kids to the internet. Where are we going to hear encouragement if not from each other?

> Do not let any unwholesome talk come out of your mouths, but only what is helpful for building others up according to their needs, that it may benefit those who listen.   EPHESIANS 4:29

We mamas are dragged down and broken into pieces every day by our whiny, grumpy kids, and we need to build each other up. Because we really do need it.

So let's lay it on thick. The mama booty pat. The nod, the smile, the you're-rocking-this-mom thing. That may be all the small talk you need to get things going.

Say Something Encouraging

Here's a suggestion about small talk. When you don't know what to say, say something encouraging. Tell her the nice thing that you were thinking in your head. Maybe you like her jeans or her daughter is a really good dribbler on the soccer team or she really nailed snack day with the peanut cocoa fudgy bars.

We have so many nice things about people running around in our heads all day and yet we walk around feeling crappy about ourselves. I made a pact with myself a few years ago that if I thought something nice about someone, then I would tell her rather than keep it to myself. It got a little awkward one day when I had to tell a stranger that she had perfect eyebrows, but darn if she hadn't perfectly plucked those luscious brows and deserved to know that someone had noticed. They were browtacular, and she had to know.

Via Twitter @UnexpectedMel

When I make something amazing for dinner I can't even be cool about it. I'm all, "Doesn't this rock your face off? Right? Best dinner ever!"

Too Deep, Too Soon

Small talk is lovely on first base, even semi-awkward compliments, but as I've learned the hard way, again and again, try to avoid going too deep, too soon. TDTS. If you can. Or, come find me, because I can't either.

I recently had a TDTS nightmare scenario play out at our local pool. We were new to the neighborhood, trying to be friendly, and we went too deep, too soon. When I say we, I really mean he. My husband, who works from home and rarely makes contact with the in-real-life outside world.

The woman sitting next to him at the pool asked him how many kids we have. That's a normal question for everyone, really. How do you mess up that question? But for those of us in the adoption process, sometimes it can be tricky. We had just put our daughter back on a plane to Latvia because we were hosting her and couldn't keep her yet. The court still had to do important things like, oh, ask her if she even wanted to be adopted by us. We had jacked-up feelings about the whole thing, and when the well-meaning neighbor asked how many kids we had, my husband proceeded to talk on and on and on.

And on and on.

And on and on.

He told her everything. On the other side of his lawn chair, I stared straight ahead trying to distance myself from the full exposure going down next to me. I told myself that if he started telling her about our kids' birth families I was going to drop something heavy on his crotch. She must've felt like she needed to disclose some of her own stuff after everything he said, so she told him about an upcoming move to another state. And then her kids joined her.

I watched the next part happen in slow motion. He asked the kids if they were looking forward to moving. The woman's face froze in panic. Her eyes widened slightly, and her kids turned to her in complete shock. *"We're moving?!?!"* At this point, I think my husband's internal organs stopped working, and I started figuring out how soon we could sell our house again. A lot of our stuff was still in boxes, after all.

Too deep, too soon. Let the relationship build. With some

friends, you'll feel a natural connection and wade into deep waters quickly. With others, it'll take time. With some, you'll be dead before it ever happens. Let it develop. Let it breathe.

Conversation Starters

Next time you find yourself needing to make a little small talk, try one of these on for size:

- How old is your child?
- Does he attend preschool?
- How long have you lived here?
- What do you like about the neighborhood/class/school?
- I'm new. What do I need to know?
- Wow, that's so awesome! Tell me more about cloth diapering/homeschooling/gluten/Jesus/your church/training for a triathlon/*Battlestar Galactica*/Spanx.
- How long have you lived in the area? Do you miss home?
- What's fun around here?
- Have you been to that pumpkin patch/bounce house/ bowling alley/children's museum?
- Do you recommend it?
- Who's your favorite Doctor? Doctor *who*? Yes, exactly.
- From where did you move?
- What's your favorite thing about being a mom?
- What's your least favorite thing about being a mom?
- Did you always think you'd be a mom or did you kinda fall into this gig?
- How do you cling to sanity in the midst of crazy kids?
- Make a positive observation about her kid: "Malcolm has such a kind heart. He's always helping the other kids in class." "Serenity's dribbling is really getting good."
- Share a recipe.

- Talk about what you cooked for dinner last night or a restaurant you tried. Everyone eats. I've never met someone who isn't at least a little interested in food.
- Saving money is another good one. If you just found a great deal on size 3T undies, by all means share it with the rest of us sitting at ballet class with our tiny dancers.

Notes

1. *The Princess Bride*, directed by Rob Reiner, Act III Communications, 1987.
2. Thanks, Amanda Mook, for bringing "booty pat" to my attention. I'm mentally booty patting you right now.

Mom Monsters

Tony Stark: "It's good to meet you, Dr. Banner. Your work on anti-electron collisions is unparalleled. And I'm a huge fan of the way you lose control and turn into an enormous green rage monster."

From *The Avengers*[1]

Have you ever met a monstrous mama? Have you ever been one? Here are some moms to watch out for, and lest you think I'm being snarky and judgmental, I have parts of all these moms in me, and you have probably been at least one of these too. And also, let's try not to be these moms. Anymore. For realsies.

The Hydra

There is possibly nothing more intimidating on this planet than groups of women who are already friends. They present as some kind of multi-headed Hydra, and it's really hard to cinch up your mom balls and present yourself to them head on ... pun totally intended. Whatever you do, don't cut off one of the heads, because two will grow back in its place and then you'll really be up poop creek.

There is possibly nothing more intimidating on this planet than groups of women who are already friends.

You can go about it a couple of different ways. First, you can try to pick off the ones on the outside. After you assess the situation, maybe you see one of the Hydra heads on the fringe not talking to anyone. That's when you sidle up to her and strike up a conversation. If you work quickly, you can get in enough conversation with her before another Hydra mom notices you, the interloper. At that point, hopefully if she has any social skills whatsoever, Hydra One will introduce you to Hydra Two and you can work your way into the belly of the beast, gathering momentum as you go.

Option two is to present yourself directly to the beast, that is, to confront the Hydra directly. It's risky and may backfire, and whereas getting shot down by one mom feels slightly awkward, getting shot down by the Hydra might leave you begging for Hercules.

I never seem to know anyone at the pool, and last year I was delighted to see the mom of one of my son's school friends. She was part of a Hydra, which I didn't realize until I walked over. I bravely went forth and engaged the Hydra. They were all very nice, but I didn't get the invitation to join them. Instead, I ended up having a tea party in the baby pool with all their kids while they planned out their weekly margarita night. Hercules!

One thing my experience with Hydras has taught me is to be that smiling head who's willing to help other moms into the fun. If you're part of a group and see a mom by herself, by Grabthar's hammer, invite her to join you.[2]

The Sphinx

This is the aggressive questioning mom. You meet her and she asks question after probing question and you have to have the right answers or she might eat you. I like to say something shocking or weird to throw her off her game and then use her surprised pause to turn the tables on her and start asking questions of my own.

Sphinx: I don't recognize you.

Me: Hi, I'm Melanie.

Sphinx: How long have you lived here? Are you from this area? What high school did you go to? Where do your kids go to school? What do you do? Are you on the Committee of Everyone Who's Completely Important? I've lived here a long time and I feel like I know everyone but I don't know you.

Me: Well, I just regenerated, so I have a new face. Heh-heh, that's a reference to *Doctor Who*, a show about a Tardis-flying Time Lord, and don't you sometimes just want to hop in a box and see the universe? I've lived here for a while but I love meeting new people. Hi! What were some of your favorite things about growing up here? What made you decide to stay here? What do you like about it? Oh, this is so exciting, like meeting one of the people who came over on the *Mayflower*. Do you know anyone who came over on the *Mayflower*? Or maybe their friends?

A version of this actually happened to me recently, although I behaved myself better because I was at church and Jesus was watching and I generally want people to like me. But in my head, just in my head, I had a great time with this lady with a key to the city. I've lived here long enough to know I can say "bless her heart."

I often go Sphinx-like on people. I like getting to know people, and if you tell me you're from another country or have any connection to adoption, I start acting like I'm trying to write your biography. I usually catch myself and try to salvage the situation by saying something like, "I'm sorry I'm asking too many questions, heh-heh. I love meeting people from other countries." *Breathe, calm down, holy cow, Mel, what's wrong with you?*

The Barnacle

Is she wearing the shirt you had on last week? Did she plagiarize your Facebook status about how with every falling leaf you say a prayer for your kids? Is that your haircut?

When you see her at the bus stop, she flags you down, performs a pick-and-roll off another mom to get you by yourself, and leeches onto you. If another mom tries to come in for some friendly banter, the Barnacle acts so off-putting that the other mom backs away and assumes that both of you are extremely weird.

She asks you for your meal plan for the week, repins your entire Pinterest board, and gets her kids to call you "Auntie" within the first week of meeting you. She is adhered to the side of your metaphorical ship and she ain't coming off.

"Imitation is the sincerest form of flattery," but there's a point when it gets creepy. If you have a friend who seems to want your identity, try to gently encourage her to discover her own. Ask her questions about what she likes and what makes her *her*, and encourage her independence.

> "Imitation is the sincerest form of flattery,"
> but there's a point when it gets creepy.

Invite her to hang out with you and a few other friends to help her plug in with other people. If she doesn't want to share you, don't stop hanging out with your other friends.

Sometimes we go through seasons when we just don't like ourselves and want to be someone else. If that someone else is you, you have an opportunity to build up another mama and help her discover her own unique personality. And if it gets too *Single White Female*, run away.

The Selfie

This mom thrives on one-upping you. She sounds like this:

Oh yeah, you think that's bad?

That's nothing, you should hear what happened to me.
The same thing happened to me, only I had twice the number of kids and double coupons.

Most of us have been guilty of this at some point, either in our heads or out our mouths. It's acceptable in small doses, like when you're exchanging baby barf stories, but in general, don't be this mom. If you encounter this mom, try kicking it up a notch and seeing if she gets the hint.

> You: Ugh, this day has been rough. Roslin bit a kid at preschool and baby Adama has his first cold.
>
> Selfie: Seriously? Don't even worry about that. My preschooler got kicked out of class for kung fu and my triplets all have a stomach virus. I've been cleaning vomit all morning long and all I had to wear was this sequined blazer.
>
> You: Oh. Well, after she bit the kid she dragged him over to the class potty, baptized him with his first swirly, and duct-taped him to the time-out chair. And the baby sneezed out a Tonka truck and I had to rush him to the ER to have his nostril stitched up. So I win.

The Pintessa

She's the same as the Selfie, only crafty. Just admit you're a loser. Don't get sucked into a competition cuz you'll lose and also end up crocheting baby booties and prune up with concealed resentment ultimately hating life and her.

If you are crafty, keep rocking it. You craft for the love of crafting, not to beat down the uncrafty. When you make something awesome, pin it. Pin the crap out of it. No shame. Your work is wonderful.

When you make something awesome,
pin it. Pin the crap out of it.

The Pintessa is the combative crafter. She's in it to win it at the kindergarten Thanksgiving feast.

You: I like your marshmallow raccoons.

Pintessa: Thanks. I used vegan marshmallows.

You: Oh! Cool.

Pintessa: I also made marshmallow snowmen, beavers, and deer.

You: Woodland animals are nice.

Pintessa: And here's the entire forest made out of homemade pretzel sticks.

You: There are five kids in the class and at the moment, three of them are picking their noses. What, am I being punked by The Food Network right now?

If you're like me and hurry to sign up for juice boxes for all your kids' events, plunk your juice boxes on the plastic-covered table, throw a compliment over your shoulder, and clear the area.

The *Besserwisser*

Besserwisser is German for "know-it-all," and we all know a mom who thinks she knows best. She's the Googler, the one who's read about everything and experienced two-thirds of it and wants to help you out. She can tell you everything you need to know about your possible irritable bowel and she'll know just the thing to get that rancid apple juice smell out of your van. She'll know exactly how you should discipline your kids, which brand of lunch meat causes brain cancer, and how many licks to get to the center of a Tootsie Pop. Sometimes you'll love her and write it all down, and sometimes you'll want to shove her smartphone down her gaping maw.

Don't be afraid to gently tell her that all you need right now is a hug. And if you realize midsentence that you're being a *Besserwisser*, it's never too late to just stop and say sorry. When I realize I'm trying to solve everyone's problems, I try to stop and say, "Oh, I'm doing that thing where I try to solve it. I'm sorry. Just want me to listen?"

I Resemble That

I catch myself resembling a little bit of all these moms from time to time. Sometimes don't you just sit back and marvel that you have any friends at all? I do. In my head when I'm hanging out with a friend, I'm thinking, *Melanie, shut up. Stop talking. Stop talking! Stop talking now! Ask her a question. Find out about her. Stop making it about you. Bleep bleepity bleep, you did it again. Cut it out!*

When it comes to friendships with other women, remember that you can't control other moms. You can only work on being the best friend you can be. I gotta say that again. *You can't control other moms. You can only work on being the best friend you can be.* And then heap on piles and piles of grace, for yourself and for them. Cuz if we're going to nail these momlationships, we're going to need it.

Notes

1. *The Avengers*, directed by Joss Whedon, Marvel Studios, 2012.
2. *Galaxy Quest*, directed by Dean Parisot, DreamWorks SKG, 1999.

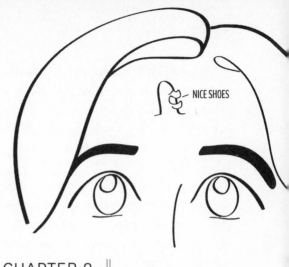
NICE SHOES

‖ CHAPTER 8 ‖

A Totally
Judgmental Zit

Ron Burgundy: "I don't know how to put this, but I'm kind of a big deal ... I have many leather-bound books and my apartment smells of rich mahogany." From *Anchorman*[1]

Have you ever trudged through a time when your family life was messy and hard? Maybe your marriage was being sucked into a black hole, or one of your kids was cracking apart, or you were struggling with depression, or even all three at one awful time?

Our adoption process with Evie took two years, and during that time, I blogged and shared and dreamed and wrote my future daughter gooey love notes on the internet for the whole world to see. I blinked on rose-colored contact lenses and just knew that all the heartache would end if we could just get her here with us. When we finally brought her home from Ethiopia, the only gooey feeling I had was the feel of the boogers streaming down my face as I sobbed over how dang hard everything was.

Adoption is beautiful and exactly the right road for our family. Our daughter is incredible and smart and funny and loving. But taking a small child who doesn't understand what's happening to her and becoming a safe place for her is a road. A long, difficult road. Attachment takes time, and the process of getting there takes a toll.

Life got insanely hard while we adjusted to this new normal of screaming, belligerent, violent, traumatized toddler. After half a year, I was a shriveled former human being. I felt like one of those blow-up Santas that people put out on their yards at Christmas. I was sad and deflated on the front lawn and someone had detached the thingy that blows in air.

All our friends, family, and acquaintances had followed our journey to our daughter. We all tend to romanticize the idea of adoption, because it's hard to acknowledge the other side, the side where there's brokenness and loss for the child. Sweet, loving people would come up to us at church and say things like, "Everything is just perfect now. All your waiting is over. It's like all the difficulty just melted away." This, after I'd spent a week in and out of doctor appointments trying to drain off the staph infection exploding from my little girl's scalp and after she'd hit me, bit me, kicked me, and used everything in her little body to let me know that she was not okay, and it felt like we'd never be okay again.

> We all tend to romanticize the idea of adoption, because it's hard to acknowledge the other side, the side where there's brokenness and loss for the child.

She had lost everything she ever knew, and even as she pushed me away, she clung to me. She pressed her face against mine, she clamored to be held every moment of the day, she sat on my lap while I pooped, and she pried open my eyelids with her sticky little fingers when I closed my eyes. With every ounce of my draining, dwindling being, I loved her, and as I drained away, I needed respite. I couldn't do this life on my own, but who would understand? I was supposed to be so happy to finally have her home. I was supposed to be a rock star, unflappable, a well-trained adoptive paragon of perfection. I was not.

Free Child Care

A friend who knew my struggle invited me to a Wednesday morning Bible study at a church that wasn't mine. I'd already attended a few worship services here and there at other churches, and I was beginning to feel like a church cheater, some kind of spiritual junkie who ran from church to church for a hit of Holy Spirit.

Whatever. This church had free child care if you went to its young moms' study on Wednesday mornings. That's all I needed to know.

It was a Methodist church, and I didn't know anything about Methodists, except that they were cool to offer free child care to nonmember, church-hopping floozies like me.

Two whole hours without the master manipulations of my sweet, angelic, completely scary daughter. I grabbed my complimentary coffee and slid into my seat as they powered up Beth Moore on the DVD player.

I wasn't there to make friends. I was there to sit by myself and hide from my daughter. And then the most horrible thing you can think of happened.

The video ended and they began circling up the chairs. *Oh, you have got to be freaking kidding me.* The chairs were blocking the doors and I couldn't decide which was worse, facing my daughter one hour early or facing these women.

They flipped the lights back on and I looked around. I judged. Oh, I did. I judged the crap out of that room full of mamas. To me, it felt like the whole room was filled with perfectly coifed women who wore adorable sandals and tucked in their shirts and had cute belts that matched their sandals.

I didn't even know where to buy the cute sandals and I was pretty sure my child was downstairs in the nursery devouring their young.

Apparently there was a discussion and prayer request section of the morning that I somehow missed in my sprint toward free child care. After checking out the room, I decided that I was a big, big freak and couldn't possibly have one thing in common with these women. I cared about poverty alleviation and orphan care and they had cute sandals.

Well, I was right about the first part. I was a big, big freak, but it turned out that half the women in there had adopted children. Several had children with special needs. Many of them volunteered regularly in serving the poor. All of them were genius rock stars with beautiful faith. I didn't know what a Methodist was, but these girls in the room with the pretty sandals knew a lot more about poverty alleviation and orphan care than I did. And they knew something about feeling like they were failing.

After working through my utter shame over being a totally judgmental zit up in my head, I ran headlong into relationship with them and kept coming back, week after week.

The poor workers in the nursery. While I was growing as a person upstairs, Evie really was devouring the room downstairs. Literally. She bit one of the sweet ladies who loved on her. And then she bit a kid. It came to a head when they had to physically remove her from the room because she wouldn't stop hitting.

Every Wednesday I'd have the best two hours of my week then slink downstairs and pick her up, cringing as I asked, "How did she do?" Bless her heart.

A couple years later and she's learned to control her inner rage monster. And I no longer judge a woman by her shoes.

She and I are both growing as people.

Judger and Judgee

It was so easy for me to size up that room and think I knew everything about those other women. When we see each other out of context of our home lives, we can assume that everyone else has it all together and we're the only ones hanging on by a thread. The truth is, so many of us are messy and cracked. We're just afraid to talk about it.

> The truth is, so many of us are messy and cracked. We're just afraid to talk about it.

We all judge other women and are judged in return. Other moms judge our kids, our parenting choices, our appearance. Even when we don't mean to, we make snap decisions about other women, and we're so dang intimidating to one another.

As a child, I spent my happy days hiding in my closet or the bathtub, reading and reading and reading. I stayed up half the night reading. My parents thought I had a personal problem because I'd lock the bathroom door and pretend to poop, for an hour, just to get in a few chapters instead of playing outside. Playing outside was like a small, allergic death.

I tried soccer and spent the majority of my time sitting at right fullback, making dandelion chains and staring at the clouds. If I ran more than three steps, my face would go beet red and I'd have a white ring around my mouth, like Bob the Tomato with a milk moustache.

I could never meet the presidential fitness tests in gym class. Who did the president think he was, making me do a pull-up? My gym teacher was appalled that I didn't know how to play baseball. (Yes, yes, I know, total irony that this book uses a baseball analogy.) And those timed races around the track, ohhh. I died. I'm pretty sure I'm non-corporeal, and my body is actually buried next to the track at my old high school.

I actually tried cross-country in eighth grade, because that's what I do. I try things. I try everything. I used my last-place position to encourage the runners around me. "You can do it! Keep going! Don't risk the embarrassment of me beating you!"

My aversion to sports has carried through to my parenting,

and I'm the world's worst soccer mom. I stand on the sidelines trying to cheer on my kids, and I do get out a few cheers in between griping that it's too hot and I wish I'd brought my chair.

I really, really like sitting. I could sit all day. I am an unabashed sitter, and I squirm when people talk about working out. Moms in spandex and running shoes completely intimidate me. To fit in, I try to throw in that time I took a step aerobics class and when I used to "trot" around the neighborhood. Can't even call what I did running. Maybe bouncing.

Via Facebook @UnexpectedMel

Volunteered at Awana tonight. Someone put me in charge of the yellow team for this thing called a relay race. There was running and a baton and I flashed back to gym class not in a good way. I tried to woo-hoo a lot to make up for my general lack of game knowledge. Woo-hoo go yellow. Run, yellow, run. I'm cold can we go inside yet?

The other day, I tried the direct approach, just letting the mom know up front what she was getting with me. I gushed about how much I loved sitting and how I could sit all day every day. I talked about sitting like people talk about pilates. She laughed and said, "That must be nice!" Yeah. It is. My butt is a little bit numb as I sit here typing, and I like it that way.

So, as a professional sitter, I'm terrified of athletic moms who talk about running and endorphins. I'm not sure what those are, but can I get them from coffee?

I'm completely intimidated by sporty women, and maybe some of them are intimidated by my competitive ability to sit. As I've gotten to know some sporties, I've found that they can be completely awesome and (a) don't judge me for my lack of coordination, and (b) don't drag me to the gym. I even have a friend who was an exercise science major. I didn't even make eye contact with those girls in college. I think they hung out in something called a field house.

The neat thing about sharing motherhood is that we don't need to have everything in common when we have our kids in common. In *Harry Potter and the Goblet of Fire*, J. K. Rowling writes, "Differences of habit and language are nothing at all if our aims are identical and our hearts are open."[2]

Whether I can run up and down a field or not, I'm watching my kids run up and down the field, and we can talk about the difficulty of yanking shin guards on a four-year-old who doesn't know how to lock his knees and help you out. (Have you ever tried this? I'm shoving and trying to explain to him how to help me by pushing his leg through the shin guard, and he's letting his leg go limp and flopping around like Raggedy Andy. I think that's about the time I call Daddy and remind him that soccer is his thing. Mommy out.)

My Own Insecurity

So I'm learning not to judge a girl by her sandals, or her spandex, and to discover the vast array of mommies being their awesome selves. When I boil it down, judgment stems from my own insecurity. I'm insecure about my lack of athletic ability, so I think sporty moms will judge me.

I'm insecure about always signing up for juice boxes at preschool, so I judge crafty moms for making cutie patootie treats they found on Pinterest. I always judge or feel judged because of my own insecurity, and as I begin to treat the root of the problem, my own self-worth and ability to love myself, I see other moms as the unique, incredible people they are.

I had to figure out that God made me and loves me for me, not because I'm trying to be someone else. My weird

Via Facebook @UnexpectedMel

When we arrived in the classroom I saw the spread of food for the party. Pinterest had barfed all over the long table. Peeled oranges and peanut butter and jelly sandwiches danced happily in the shape of little pumpkins. Orange Rice Krispie treat balls sported Tootsie Roll stems. Green chocolate-dipped Frankenstein marshmallows with hair sprinkles grinned up at me on sticks. They were judging me.

sense of humor, my love of sitting, my need to front hug everyone. He loves me. A basic, Sunday-school-level truth that I'm still trying to learn in my mid-thirties.

And he loves you. Oh so much.

> My friend and I were each other's non-judgmental support systems and when we would completely bomb at our mothering duties and give our children yet another thing to have to share with a therapist one day, we knew we could call the other and hear words of encouragement and acceptance. Isn't that what so much of our fears boil down to anyway? Acceptance? We long to know, not just from our spouse but also from other women, that we are accepted and loved for who we are. That when you strip away the trendy clothes, the makeup, the latest parenting technique, the crafty crafter, the beautifully decorated house, the seemingly perfect marriage, and all the other things we judge ourselves and others on, what is left is good enough, stretch marks and all. It did not necessarily come naturally to be so unabashedly honest, but it was worth it. — *Carolyn M.*

Well. If we've practiced our small talk, avoided monsters and being monstrous, and have squelched any insecure judgery, we might be ready to try second base. Shall we?

A Note on Base-Jumping

"Even though we've only talked at Trinity's jujitsu lessons, I really like her and just want to invite her over."

Let's talk about base-jumping. A lot of people do this, including me. If you really click with another mom and your daughters are hugging it out in the parking lot of gymnastics class or your sons are doing that boy thing where they beat the crap out of each other in an "I love you, man" kind of way, then yes, consider base-jumping.

Base-jumping works well if you sense that you guys share similar parenting styles and she'll roll with it if your kid decides to strip naked and streak through the kitchen when she's mid-sip of your relaxing chamomile tea with local honey. If I'm unsure about how the other mama feels about me or my kids, I stick to running the bases and don't try to steal third.

Sometimes you just know. After several soccer practices, you throw out a quote from *Monty Python and the Holy Grail* and she lobs one right back. Oh. It is on. You're just thinking, *How fast can I get her back to my place?* And that's when you're ready for base-jumping.

Unless you're planning on base-jumping all your momlationships, let's now proceedeth to second, not third. Fourth is right out.

Notes

1. *Anchorman*, directed by Adam McKay, DreamWorks, 2004.

2. J. K. Rowling, *Harry Potter and the Goblet of Fire*. (New York: Scholastic Press, 2000), 723.

Part 2

SECOND BASE

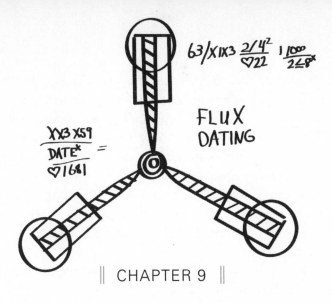

FLUX
DATING

$\dfrac{XX3 \times X5\eta}{DATE^*} = \heartsuit 16\&1$

$63/X1X3 \dfrac{2/4^2}{\heartsuit 22} | \dfrac{1000}{2\angle 8^x}$

|| CHAPTER 9 ||

Dating on the Space-Time Continuum

Doc: "The encounter could create a time paradox, the results of which could cause a chain reaction that would unravel the very fabric of the space-time continuum, and destroy the entire universe!" *From Back to the Future Part II*[1]

Okay, you've made first base. Breathe. You've gone to Girl Scouts/ football practice/Baby Big Brain Music Class, forced yourself to talk, and amazingly, scored a great new friend prospect or two. What's next?

If making a phone call or sending an email does not come naturally to you, there are still some ways to reach out. As you're finishing up at the first-base group/meeting/game, propose a playdate and throw out a day and time. By tacking it on at the end of your time together, you already have the context in which to bring it up and it keeps the momentum going. Your acquaintance will immediately know that you enjoyed her company and that you want to get to know her better.

Another option is to immediately piggyback right off of a first-base date. If you've just finished up music class with a group of moms and kids, ask a few if they want to grab lunch or ice cream and let the kids keep playing at Mc-fil-A-King's playland.

However you initiate the next playdate, make sure you lock it down. How many times have you met a mom and fallen prey to the "Oh yeah, we should so totally get together" cycle that never ends? Every time you see each other, one of you says that, but no one ever gets anything on the calendar, and months down the road, you're still shoulding all over each other.

I take my cue from my four-year-old daughter, who is constantly trying to lock me into a plan.

Evie: When are we going to the zoo?

Me: We'll go soon.

Evie: When?

Me: I'm not sure. I'm good for it. Don't worry.

Evie: In the morning?

Me: Soooooonnnnn.

Evie: When? Tomorrow? Tomorrow in the morning?

She would schedule out our entire month, complete with meals, if I let her. I've had to start telling her I make no commitments until after I have my coffee in the morning.

Location, Location, Location

If you're on second base, location is critical. When choosing a venue, you want one with several options, plenty of space, the ability to get loud, and escape routes. I'm a hopeless case, but I try to give my mini-weirdos the chance to make the best impression they possibly can.

Before I had a mobile child, I was a total idiot about this. My little babe would quietly suck on my boob and I didn't understand the whole world of toddlers and kids who could move and talk. I invited my friends to places like Starbucks and the quiet tearoom in our town where the tables were made of toothpicks and everything could shatter if you breathed on it wrong. My precious Rose, who actually met me for lunch there, is the kindest, most tolerant person on the planet. She should've called me a moron and moved on. Instead, she managed squirmy, mobile children in a room filled with china while I blindly sipped my tea and talked about how tired I was. Dude. She must've really liked me.

If someone invites you to a location that you know will put your kids on their worst behavior, it's totally okay to suggest a different location. Provide a little explanation, so they don't just think you're a high-maintenance control freak. For instance, we are now in the land of food intolerances and I have a limited number of eating-out options. At home we eat weird things like brown rice crackers and coconut yogurt, and if I'm really feeling like a party, I'll pull out the faux Oreos that taste like grout.

If a friend recommends a restaurant that means I'll have to pack our food and wipe the tears out of my son's eyes while the other kids eat ice cream in front of him, I explain that we have some issues with gluten and dairy. If you want to protect your child's privacy, you don't have to offer a long explanation. Just a casual, "Could we go here instead? We have a few allergies and this other place has several things we can eat."

Parks are great, though I've found that if you want to get to know the other mom at all, pick a park that isn't that crowded and only has one way to leave. We have a fabulous park in our town that the kids love, but I never choose it when I'm trying to hang out with another mom, because it's ginormous, has several exits, is next to a lake, and has a field of geese that like to nip.

Whenever we go there, the kids run in opposite directions, want to hang out on the edge of the water, and fail to safely navigate the goose poop land mines. Oh, and there's a fountain. So we have water-soaked kids with poop on their shoes who are scattered all over tarnation and possibly drowning in the lake.

I don't mind parenting that scenario, but I can't try to make a new friend at the same time. Oh, and there's no shade. In Georgia. I suffer from heat-induced, Hulk-like rage syndrome, so I'm not going to make my best impression with my eyeballs frying on my face. Know thyself.

> I'm not going to make my best impression
> with my eyeballs frying on my face.
> ====================

I like the parks where there's a bench that overlooks the whole thing, nothing else to do except play at the park, and loads of wide-open spaces for frolicking and malarkey. Mom friend and I can slide to second base together while the kiddos play safely and within my peripheral gaze. And shade.

If you have littles who are stroller-compatible, taking a walk is another great second-base option. After we brought our daughter home from Ethiopia, I met friends each week to walk around the lake. One of them is so in shape that the only way I could keep up was for her to wear her toddler while pushing her three-year-old in the stroller while pregnant with her third child. Yeah. And I was still panting. (You already know I'm not this fit, athletic mama, so honestly, we only walked around the lake a handful of times and I don't think I've exercised since.)

When you're a mom, most of your dates are doubles or triples . . . with your kids. I have been to the zoo, hung out at the house, and grocery shopped with other moms. My friend and I used to walk miles and miles multiple times a week while pushing our kids in strollers. We were so diligent and kept each other accountable during the times so many people don't even want to be outside. We walked in the rain a few times, dead cold of winter, and hot sweaty summer. We pushed ourselves to go farther, a record at twelve miles, and even ran some days. Now when you're exercising you don't wear cute clothes, unless you're one of those moms and I'm not judging but I sweat too much to care about coordinating my running skirt with my sweat-wicking tank, visor, and neon pink running shoes . . . We wear T-shirts, Nike shorts, sweat pants, mismatched socks, oversized hoodies, dirty hair pulled back in ponytails only getting dirtier. And it didn't matter because we got hours of quality time talking about life and family and enduring those last couple of miles together when our feet were killing us and our kids wanted to kill us because enough with the stroller already. — *Kim T.*

We have a dive of a pizza shop in town with carpet that's older than I am. In the back, they have a small game room with no exits filled with mostly broken arcade games and a bathroom. I love this place, because once I scope out the bathroom and make sure it's pedophile-free, my kids have a fun zone for shenanigans away from the eyeball rolls of grown-ups out for grown-up luncheons. (It's just lunch unless you're kid-free. Then it's a luncheon. And my pizza dive might not qualify in the luncheon category, with or without kids.)

When my kids were really little, the magic pizza dive was even better because the blinking lights of the games mesmerized them into thinking that's all they did. One day when an older kid laden with quarters showed up and made the games come alive, my cover was blown and I had to ante up or skip the pizza joint.

Wherever you go, in or out, you want options. If your child starts to melt down, you want to be somewhere where you can provide something else to do. Here's a ball, here's sidewalk chalk, have some bubbles, let's move into this room over here, time to pull out our picnic lunch. Distract distract distract fun fun jazz hands.

Impromptu Second Base

Once in a while, you may stumble onto a temporal rift in the space-time continuum, and you don't have to lift a texting finger to create the date. For example, one day I took the kids out for lunch after school. As they raced toward the indoor playland, they saw that two of their friends from school were already there and playing together. They immediately sat down with their friends. As I walked over with our food, I realized that the two moms were also sitting together. We'd smiled and exchanged pleasantries at class parties and open houses, but I'd never laid eyes on them outside of school. This was the moment. We were out of the classroom and in a neutral location. Would they ask me to join them? Would I say yes? Hello, impromptu second base. I didn't see you coming, but I welcome you.

Moms are amazing creatures. In the right situation, we love to share. Before we'd even finished our nuggets and fries, we were talking adoption and epidurals, surgeries and inductions. In an hour, we moved from "hi/bye" acquaintances to friends. They offered to help with my kids when we traveled to pick up our new daughter in Latvia, and they didn't seem to mind when I made references to both the *Lord of the Rings* and *Doctor Who*.

Me: Your daughter's name is Rohan?!?! As in "Riders of"? That is So. Cool.

Her: Uhh ...?

Me: *Lord of the Rings*? The Horse Lords? King Theoden? The Battle of Helm's Deep?

Her: I haven't seen that movie—

Me: The book—

Her: Or read the book.

Me: I'm really weird.

Her: No, it's okay!

Me: "The battle for Helm's Deep is over; the battle for Middle Earth is about to begin." Sorry, I'm done.

At this point we really need to talk about group dates. Group dates are tricky beasts, because they lack the intimacy of third base but can occur in someone's house, which is definitely not neutral territory. Whether they're in a home or out in the world, group dates are a valuable tool for developing relationships without all the pressure of a one-on-one. Sometimes the best way to get to know other moms is to practice "safety in numbers," so let's get to it.

Notes

1. *Back to the Future Part II*, directed by Robert Zemeckis, Universal Pictures, 1989.

‖ CHAPTER 10 ‖

The Group Date

Rex: "At Rex Kwan Do, we use the buddy system. No more flying solo. You need somebody watching your back at all times." *From Napoleon Dynamite*[1]

A great way for your kids to have fun and get that ever-important socialization while you get to know a whole bunch of people is The Group Date. Group dating is great, because it's not up to two people to keep the conversation going and you're more likely to find things in common with someone when there are several someones in the room.

I have both attended and hosted group dates, and if you've been to one and it was bad, try, try again. My first group date was pleasant enough, but all the moms went to the same pediatrician and talked about how giving your kids cow's milk was a no-no. On the outside, I was smiling and enjoying the conversation, but on the inside I was freaking out and trying to figure out how I felt about all this new anti-dairy information. I decided that anti-dairy talk stressed me out and I didn't go back. Ironic, since four years later I went dairy-free. I should really go look those girls up....

Jaws: Not the Movie

A couple of years ago when my husband took a bro-trip to Uganda, I decided to keep myself busy by hosting a group date for twenty people. It just kept getting bigger and bigger. As moms and kids streamed into my house, I offered to make lunch for everyone. I'm a whimmy kind of person and don't plan for these things, so I looked in the pantry and pulled out my one jar of fancy Williams Sonoma simmer sauce and went to town on some chicken and rice. It was a fishes and loaves scenario, because there was probably enough for six people but I just kept ladling. Of course, Jesus probably made bigger portions, whereas mine were more like those chicken samples on a toothpick you get at the mall.

Everyone was having a great time, and there were kids everywhere. I was feeling really great about myself until the screaming started. In my house, we are all loud, like, all the time. Just really, really loud people. And I tend to hang out with loud people from loud homes. LOUDLY. So for screaming to catch my attention, well, you can imagine the decibel level one would have to achieve. My friend Clara's daughter came shrieking down the stairs with bite marks on her forehead. You could've made retainers from these perfect dental impressions. I marched upstairs looking for the culprit, and there he was, the boy who earned the nickname "Jaws" when he was in the one-year-old class at church. My son.

My house was filled with a vast array of all my friends, I'd just served a fancy, extremely schmansy gourmet lunch, and now my boy had taken a chunk out of someone's head. Elliott just could not make that girl back off and give him space, so he used his teeth.

Anybody know that level of desperation when your kid does something so horrible in front of your friends? Discipline is a must. You have the pressure of eyeballs staring at you, and you have to think so lightning-bolt fast to handle the whole thing with grace, poise, strength, dignity, and firmness.

I wanted to bite the little bugger back. I didn't.

Thankfully, Clara is one of my closest friends, we know each other's junk, we completely adore each other, and we forgive each other's kids for being the punks that they are. If this story had been about the chewed-up child of a second-base friend, well, we may not have recovered. And you'd be scared off from group dates forever. I think we can deduce two important points from the story: (a) know your child's limits and (b) sometimes things go painfully and awkwardly wrong.

> I joined a Facebook social group for moms in Tauranga, New Zealand, and had seen that someone else had introduced herself saying she was new to town and wanted to meet some other moms. She had quite a few replies with lots of mums wanting to meet up for a coffee and playdate. I decided to add myself to the party! "Hi, I'm new too. Can I come along?" Everyone was quite welcoming, and so far I've met someone in the group who is my age and is someone I just clicked with, and it's a good start. Thank God for social media! — *Julie M.*

Hosting a Group Date

If you've decided to host a group date, good! And on behalf of all dating moms, thank you for initiating and getting us all together. First, don't freak out about your house. Don't freak out about your house. Don't freak out about your house.

One time I had someone tell me that she felt like she needed to paint her baseboards before she could have the neighbors over. Uh, I didn't exactly know what a baseboard was at the time, and I definitely wasn't going to paint mine. Don't freak out about your house! If you have a friend who would judge you about your house, then that's her issue, not yours, and you've given her a super awesome opportunity to grow. Also, the size of your house doesn't matter. Let me say that again. Size doesn't matter.

Before everyone comes over, get your house straight enough for kids to have room to dump out all your toys, and designate a place for the moms to sit together. We moms are used to sitting on floors, and just sitting anywhere having adult conversation is a special treat. So don't worry about crampiness or having a dedicated playroom.

Keep snacks simple. Unless you love to cook and plan menus, in which case have at it and invite me. But if you're busy and tired and just trying to get together with some friends, don't worry about entertaining. In *A Life That Says Welcome*, Karen Ehman writes about offering hospitality, not entertainment. She says:

> *Entertaining puts the emphasis on you and how you can impress others. Offering hospitality puts the emphasis on others and strives to meet their physical and spiritual needs so that they feel refreshed, not impressed, when they leave your home.*[2]

That simple idea flipped the purpose of my gatherings around. Early on, I loved to entertain. I spent time on pretty finger foods and worked to make the details perfect. Inviting people over took work, because I looked at it as entertaining.

When I started practicing hospitality, having people over became more about blessing them and less about the compliments I received. Now when moms come over, I offer them something to drink and I might have a couple bowls of snacks out, but I focus my time on conversation, not on bustling around the kitchen. I keep mini tacos in the freezer so that when our morning together creeps toward lunch and we don't want it to end, I have a go-to lunch option for our kids that lets us spend another hour together.

If you're hosting a group date, make introductions. I'm completely terrible at introducing everyone to everybody. I tend to assume that everyone knows everyone, which can leave my friends standing there awkwardly playing eyeball tag. If you know two of the moms have something in common, tell them that when you introduce them. As I mentioned earlier, I met one of my dearest friends at a group date when we discovered that we both struggled with infertility. The hostess was a rockin' matchmaker and thought we'd hit it off. She was right.

Other Kinds of Group Dates

Of course I've mainly described group playdates here where the kids are involved, but there are many, many other ways and excuses to get together with a group sans kids. And don't forget to invite women without kids. While I watched my friends have babies without me, I was so thankful for the ones who continued to include me at a time when I struggled to belong. (While dating without kids is really fourth-base material, in this section, I'm talking about the less intimate group settings, which are excellent opportunities to chat up potential close friends.)

Who knows, you might meet your new best friend, mom or otherwise, at a Pampered Chef feast, an Ornaments4Orphans Christmas party, a Creative Memories scrapbooking night, a Noonday trunk show, or any number of other sit-and-be-sold-to parties.

And don't forget the classic book group. The nice thing about a book group is that (a) there's something to talk about; (b) you take turns hosting; and (c) it meets regularly so you don't have the work of checking everyone's schedules to see if they can make it.

A few years ago, I realized I was stuck in a reading rut and needed to break into other genres, so I invited everyone I knew and everyone they knew to a monthly book club. I got to know other moms in town and the book club helped us talk about things besides parenting. We took turns choosing the books and had the delightful chance to get to know each other as women and readers, discovering what we liked about books, authors, and ideas.

There's only one thing better than a group of moms coming together for a snack 'n' chat—a group of moms coming together to help others who are struggling on the journey.

Notes

1. *Napoleon Dynamite*, directed by Jared Hess, Fox Searchlight Pictures, 2004.
2. Karen Ehman, *A Life That Says Welcome: Simple Ways to Open Your Heart & Home to Others* (Grand Rapids: Revell, 2006), 18.

CHAPTER 11

Moms Can
Change the World

Derek Zoolander: "There's more to life than being really, really, really good looking. Right, kids?" *From Zoolander*[1]

I love so many things about moms coming together, and in addition to the benefits to us as women and to our families, we also can move mountains, break chains, and shine a light that radiates through our dark, dark world. Here are some ideas for your next group date that are fun for you and the kids, and will impact mamas and kiddos around *your* world and around *the* world.

Collection for a Cause

I have a friend in town who hosts fabulous group dates, and they don't stop at simply getting moms and kids together. When she emails to invite everyone over, she also invites everyone to bring something for an organization to bless kids in need. One time it was toiletries for a local shelter, and we piled up packages of tissues and toilet paper on her porch on our way into her house.

At the beginning of the school year, she had a back-to-school group date and we all brought school supplies, which she donated to a local organization collecting them for children living in poverty. At Christmas, she had us over again, and we brought items to pack shoeboxes. Each mom brought a lot of one item, and we got to know each other better while our kids rode their bikes in the cul-de-sac. While we chatted, we created an assembly line and packed boxes filled with soap, toothbrushes, small toys, and school supplies for Operation Christmas Child.

On several occasions, I've organized group playdates "for a cause." My thinking is usually, "Well, it's always fun to get together with all the kiddos AND we have a hard time by ourselves doing service projects, so, why not do it all at once?" A fun one was organizing a group to pack shoeboxes for Operation Christmas Child. Everyone brought their own boxes and enough of one item to fill everyone else's box with that item. Yes, it involved a lot of logistics, but that's the beauty of Evite! We moms talked the time away as we packed the boxes. A few industrious older kids helped with the packing, but most of the younger ones just had a great afternoon playing with their friends. (Except for my three-year-old, who screamed long and hard when he realized that not ONE of the goody-filled boxes was for him!) We have such little free time as moms, so why not maximize it by doing something we don't often get the chance to do? And most of us are good at multi-tasking, so we can watch our kids, catch up with a friend, and pack a shoebox (or whatever) at the same time! – *Elizabeth H.*

Shoe-Cutting Party

My friend Rory first told me about Sole Hope when we were in Uganda together playing with barefoot children. We joke that our Uganda trip together actually was our first date. If that was first, I'm not really sure what base we're on at this point. I like to think of her as the left hemisphere of my brain, because, well, I don't really have one of those.

I started following Sole Hope on Twitter, and after their eleventy-hundredth tweet about coffee, I decided they were totally fabulous. I met Asher Collie, the founder of Sole Hope, at a conference, and her passion for the people of Uganda is inspiring. Using recycled milk jugs and old jeans, Sole Hope enlists people here to cut shoe materials, which are then stitched by Ugandan stitchers in their employ. The soles of the Sole Hope shoes are made from recycled tires, so the whole project from start to finish is upcycling at its finest, and life-changing for the kids and families receiving the shoes. The finished shoes slide onto the feet of children suffering from jiggers, a sand flea that lays eggs inside the toes. Asher and her team train families in Uganda on how to safely remove jiggers, decreasing the spread of HIV and future foot trauma. I've thrown a few shoe parties for Sole Hope, and they are a fabulous way to get together with friends and make a difference for families in Uganda.

Sole Hope walks you through the process, which utilizes materials that you already have lying around your house. I love this process, because we get to enter into some seriously awesome work while gabbing with our friends. At one party, we sang show tunes and danced around, and at another, we had deeper conversations than ever before. As our hands stayed busy, we shared the stories of our lives, and it was amazing to get to know each other in a way that couldn't happen just sitting in a circle and staring at one another. Put a pair of scissors in someone's hands and she'll tell you her life story. Love this.

Caring for Foster Care

My husband and I recently attended foster care training to find out more about how we can help kids in our own county. As I've spoken with foster moms, I've discovered that when a child goes into care, she arrives with very little, maybe a small trash bag of items. Can you imagine having strangers remove you from your home in the middle of the night and take you to a new house without any of your things?

One idea for a group date is to pack backpacks for kids coming into foster care. Collect backpacks, fuzzy blankets, pajamas, teddy bears, and other comforting items and get together with friends to assemble everything. We have a group of foster parents at our church, and I'm working on putting this together with friends so that every time one of the families brings home a child, we can get a backpack to them.

Children love their names. They love hearing their names, seeing their names on signs, searching for their names. I think a powerful way to bless a child in foster care is to give him or her something personalized. One foster mom I know told me of a group that did a swimsuit and towel project in the spring, embroidering names on towels. Each child in care received an embroidered towel and a swimsuit just in time for summer. Water bottles are a great idea too, and you can use stickers or paint to personalize those as well. This is where Pinterest-loving moms can really shine. Go nuts and make it awesome.

If you're interested in what you can do to help foster kids in your area, AdoptUSKids provides state-specific information. This organization offers resources for how to get involved with things like respite care, mentoring, and even helping with photography and videography. Foster moms work hard, and I love the idea of all of us mamas pooling together to support them and the kids they serve.

I am very task-oriented, so when I can come up with a productive idea to spend time with friends, while doing something to serve others, I run with it. What amazes me is how willing my friends are to jump in and help when I take on a new project. Whether it is sewing dresses for children in Uganda, food drives for our community food bank, or coordinating service projects for our children to accomplish, my awesome friends are ready to donate, lend a hand, or volunteer. All I have to do is ask! — *Julie P.*

Cupcakes and Running

My friend works with an organization that advocates for child prisoners in Uganda. Due to lack of resources, children who come in contact with the law, whether they've broken a law or need care and protection, are taken into prisons and remain there until their cases are brought to trial or long-term solutions are established. Sixty Feet provides short- and long-term care and raises money for lawyers to go over and represent the kids in court.

Their mission is amazing and nothing to laugh at, but I can't help snickering at her Facebook posts, because the two ways they raise money are through cupcakes and running. Anyone care to guess which one appeals to me? I "like" every cupcake post and try to scroll past the running ones before they rub off on me.

But within this one organization, Sixty Feet, we have two amazing group-date opportunities for our gamut of girlfriends. You can get together with friends, everybody bring their favorite cupcake recipe, and blow up someone's kitchen with the power of flour. Then set up a cupcake stand and sell the cupcakes for Cupcake Kids. Pinterest moms, get your fondant on.

And then there's the running. For you sporterrific friends, grab your girls, don matching kneesocks, and head out to a 5K to raise money for children wrongly imprisoned. Run Sixty Feet will set you up with all the tools you need to make your kilometers count, and all the money you raise will go to help the kids in Uganda. Those of us non-sporties will watch your kids for you. Yeah, you heard me. I'd rather flippin' watch everyone's kids than run outside in nature.

Letter-Writing Party

If you have a group of friends that wants to get involved with helping orphans and vulnerable children, check out Children's HopeChest for how you can all sponsor kids in the same orphanage or village and work as a group to make a difference in an entire community. As a Sponsorship Coordinator for HopeChest, I have the privilege of meeting and working with hundreds of sponsors for the kids in our program. These awesome people pay a monthly fee to provide nutrition, medical care, education, and spiritual support for the kids living in the village, with the long-term goal of sustainability so they don't even need us anymore.

Paying the money is just part of it. The relationship between sponsor and child is the catalyst for life change. These kids are amazing, and like the kids living in our homes, they need to hear that we're believing in them, praying for them, and rooting for them.

One thing I hear from sponsors is the struggle to write letters. Many people aren't sure what to write, and even I struggle with this sometimes, even though I've met my sponsored children several times.

Whether you sponsor a child through Children's HopeChest or another sponsorship program, a fabulous group date activity is to have a letter-writing and card-making date. Lay out supplies and have ideas, sample letters, and topics on index cards around the room. You can have a kids' table and an adult table or mix everybody together.

Make sure everyone arrives with the name, ID number, and location of their child, and make sure all cards and letters are labeled correctly. You can provide envelopes and stamps, or have people bring their own.

At the end of the date, you'll have a big stack of love to send to some kiddos around the world. Follow your sponsorship program's instructions for mailing the letters.

When mamas get together, we don't just enjoy our lives more. We can make a difference in the world. One mom caring can change a family. A group of moms caring can change a community.

> One mom caring can change a family. A group
> of moms caring can change a community.

Notes

1. *Zoolander*, directed by Ben Stiller, Paramount Pictures, 2001.

CHAPTER 12

How Not to Choke on Your Own Foot

Dr. Frederick Frankenstein: "You know, I'm a rather brilliant surgeon. Perhaps I can help you with that hump."
Igor: "What hump?"   From *Young Frankenstein*[1]

Not everyone is going to like you.

It's a painful truth that I continue to tell myself. Not everyone is going to like me. Not every mom I meet is going to be my new fourth-base bestie. When I allow myself to be myself from the very beginning, there's a natural weeding-out process that occurs as other women realize how weird I am. And it's okay.

Not everyone's going to like you; however, it is possible to be yourself without alienating the people around you. I don't know about you, but there are those days when I feel like Melanie Dale, Offender of the Universe. My foot gets lodged so far into my mouth that I think I'm going to choke on it. Or now that everyone texts, my foot gets lodged in my thumbs.

So, we be ourselves. And, here are some ways not to choke on your own foot.

Wow That's So Awesome

Anytime you start getting to know someone, unless you talk exclusively about chirping birdies and fluffy cumulous clouds, inevitably you will encounter her opinions on everything from religion to food allergies to what you should or should not watch on Netflix. When this happens and I'm faced with a particularly fervent opinion, I use the "wow that's so awesome" approach. Not that you're going to agree with their blood sacrifices to the god Molech, but when you're listening about how, oh, say gluten-free/dairy-free has completely changed their lives, you can still think it's awesome that they've found something that works AND happily chug the Cheez-Its box from Sam's Club.

I experience massive levels of humility every single day since going gluten-free and dairy-free with my son two years ago. He needed to, and I decided to do it with him to be supportive. Within a couple of weeks, both of us felt like different people. That sounds fabulous, right? Who wouldn't want to feel better?

The downside to all this dietary experimentation is that I found myself in the unusual position of explaining our nutritional decisions whenever we went anywhere with another family. My mom dates, which used to include frozen pizza and gargantuan quantities of brownies and ice cream, became me answering questions about our new lifestyle. I realized how much pride I had in being the low-maintenance friend, and now I was The Ruiner of All Fun and my kid was sobbing as he watched other kids eat Twizzlers.

I really appreciate the moms in my life who take the "wow that's so awesome" approach with me. They don't feel threatened by our weird eating habits, and I have the freedom to make the choices I need to make without spending a lot of time discussing it.

I use this approach with more than just food. I ask questions about homeschooling and think it's completely amazing and awesome and love hanging out with my friends who are passionate about it, AND, we don't currently do that.

And "wow that's so awesome" tell me about how you do or don't do Santa and "wow that's so awesome" about your incredible chore charts. I sincerely love hearing how other moms do things, and I try to get excited and be supportive, even if they do things differently than I do.

Phrasing Is Everything

We can listen well, and we can also share our own lives and opinions in a way that builds bridges, rather than walls. You should avoid "you should" statements, because they can immediately put the other mom on the defensive (See what I did there?). Whether it's our dietary needs or our cloth diapering choices, I struggle with feeling annoying. If I mention it, I feel like the other mom thinks I'm judging her for not making those choices. I'm not, so if I need to bring it up, I try to say it in a funny or self-deprecating way.

> **Via Twitter @UnexpectedMel**
>
> If one more person counsels me to enjoy every minute because the time goes fast, I Will Flip Out On You.

Here are two different ways that I could talk about cloth diapering. Which one is more annoying?

You should cloth diaper. It's better for the environment and my kids never have diaper rash.

My kids wear cloth diapers. My minivan just smells better when there's poop in a Ziploc sitting in the sun. No, seriously, I wanted to try it and it seems to have helped my son's diaper rash, but it's not for everyone.

Don't you want to just throw a dirty diaper *at* me with the first one? I would completely deserve it. Phrasing is everything. I bristle when people tell me what I should do or need to do, but when they're just talking about what's worked for them, I lean in and I want to know more.

Say You're Sorry

The other key to prying your foot out of your mouth is to say you're sorry. At some point you're going to say the wrong thing, and if you're like me, it's going to be sooner rather than later. We all have those topics that make us foam at the mouth a little and get us all worked up. For me, it's orphan advocacy.

I can't quit talking. I just keep going. My voice climbs louder and louder until I'm orating in the Colosseum in my toga and sandals and then I'm Doc Brown and my hair is sticking up and I'm freaking out about the flux capacitor and I'm Hamlet and it's to be or not to be a sponsor for one of the kids I'm pushing on you and I'm trying to act all cool but I haven't blinked in like forever and my contacts are getting crispy on the edges and why won't I stop talking?

You know when you've said too much or the wrong thing. And you know what you should do. Like we tell our kids, "Say you're sorry." It's horrible and sweaty and shaky, but the more you do it, the easier it gets. If I think I've said anything that could be taken the wrong way, I try to follow up with the person to apologize.

If it's just a little thing, a text is fine, but if you can tell you offended her and there's any chance tone could be misconstrued, just pick up the phone. Make sure she can hear the tone of your voice. Usually, as soon as you go to apologize, the other person is quick to say it's okay and your friendship will be stronger for it, because you've shown that even though you hurt her, you care enough about her to make it right and pursue her.

And if someone takes the time to go through the sweaty, shaky apology, you have to forgive. You have to. And if it's the third time she's apologizing for wrecking your car, maybe you just don't give her the keys anymore.

> Therefore, as God's chosen people, holy and dearly loved,
> clothe yourselves with compassion, kindness, humility, gentle-
> ness and patience. Bear with each other and forgive one another
> if any of you has a grievance against someone. Forgive as the

Lord forgave you. And over all these virtues put on love, which binds them all together in perfect unity.

COLOSSIANS 3:12–14

That's beautiful. And sometimes it's a lot harder in real life than on the little vellum Bible page. Clothe. Bear. Forgive.

Brilliant, Genius, Awesome Focus

In college, one of my British Literature classes was taught by a British professor. Every time I'd answer a question, he would say, "Brilliant." I started thinking, "Wow, he thinks I'm brilliant. I rock *Beowulf.* I so rock this class." Then I discovered that he used "brilliant" like I use "awesome." I don't actually mean that you fill me with awe on a scale up there with the Creator of the universe. And my professor didn't mean that I was shining like the sun or even Mensa-level smart. Still, hearing that I was brilliant every day made me love him, myself, and the class, at least until I had to deconstruct *The Canterbury Tales* as a socialist manifesto. Then I was done, dropped my English major, and went to hide in the theatre with all the normal people.

I have several friends who always make me feel amazing. When I started thinking about what it was that made it so encouraging to talk with them, I realized that their way of listening was so enthusiastic that it made me excited about my life and what God was up to. These girls have the power to take someone from anxious and unsure to jazzed and ready.

I have a friend who constantly says, "Dude. That's so genius. Dude. Genius." Now, let's suspend our disbelief that anything I come up with could possibly be genius. She makes me feel like what I'm saying matters, to her, even if not to the world.

And another friend is similar. She's oh-so-wise, has six kids, and has this uncanny ability to focus solely on you while her house is on fire. She'll sit down, give you total focus, and shake her head a little, saying, "That's. So. Awesome." As people come in and out and her phone goes off, she stays focused. For those minutes together, she is yours. She pulls me into her space station with her powerful tractor beam, locking on and not letting go.

So we're listening well, and we're also focusing. When I started dating moms with my one little sleepy baby, I had no idea how hard this was. My friends with multiple kids who all talked over each other all the livelong day could not finish a thought to save their lives. I was a linear person who wanted to start at the beginning and end at the end and work my way sequentially through a topic, but that was impossible with my new mommy-brained friends. And now that I also have all of the talkers with all of the words at me, I understand and no longer feel the need — wait, what was I writing about?

Via Twitter @UnexpectedMel

This morning I couldn't spell refrigerator. Good-bye sixth grade spelling champ. Hello mommy brain.

To help with the limited amount of focus available to mommy brain, I try to keep my phone out of the way on dates. For those of us with kids in school or high-level cabinet appointments, we do need to be reached in an emergency, so I'm not saying dunk your phone in a water glass or leave it in the car, just keep it close enough that you can hear it but not so close that you're checking it over and over.

If your kids keep coming up and interrupting your friend, have them wait until she's finished her thought before you find out what they need, unless there are torrents of blood. I give my kids the finger. That is, the pointer finger held up at their faces until my friend finishes and then they can get it out politely.

Years ago, I taught my son to lightly tap me on the arm to let me know he needed to tell me something. As he's grown, his taps have gotten heavier, and recently I've had to talk with him about punching Mommy in the arm over and over. Dude, genius, but not cool.

Notes

1. *Young Frankenstein*, directed by Mel Brooks, Gruskoff/Venture Films, 1974.

|| CHAPTER 13 ||

Wield Your Weirdness
Like a Boss

Gordie: "Do you think I'm weird?"

Chris: "Definitely."

Gordie: "No man, seriously, am I weird?"

Chris: "Yeah, but so what? Everybody's weird."

From *Stand By Me*[1]

This chapter could also be titled "Be Yourself." The older I get, the easier it is for me to do just that.

A few years into our marriage, my husband called me clumsy. What. Ever. As. If.

I indignantly informed him where he could gently insert his onerous assertion. Ridiculous. I was nimble like a ninja. I was Crouching Tiger Kung Fu Panda. I could bungee dance from the ceiling like Lara Croft, fly through the air like Trinity, and high kick like Buffy.

Flash forward to the present.

Either he's some kind of prophetic genius or he saw something in me that I was unwilling to admit.

I'm ridiculously clumsy. I turn that word into onomatopoeia. *Clump! See?*

I'm constantly coming up with new ways to injure myself, like when I was lying in bed with my iPhone above my head. I fumbled the phone and dropped it squarely on my face. Has anyone ever in the history of smartphones done something as dumb as this?

One time I cut my finger on a piece of dried hash brown. I think this one actually speaks to both my clumsiness to snag my finger on a *pan* and also my disgusting proclivity of leaving the dinner dishes till the morning. A hash brown needs a lot of drying time to develop a razor-sharp edge able to lacerate an index finger.

Soon after we moved into our new house with the basement and new set of deadly steps, Alex found me lying at the bottom of them, still holding my coffee cup, of course, because it would take an act of God to get me to drop that.

I veered into the left lane while driving when I tried to adjust the visor and clocked myself in the forehead with it. Thankfully, I was in a parking lot, but I think the guy coming toward me laughed.

If You Can't Fix It, Feature It

We had a saying in theatre: if you can't fix it, feature it.[2] For example, if there's a big pole in the middle of the stage and you can't get rid of it without the roof caving in, make the pole an important part of the set design.

I can't seem to fix my clumsiness, so now I feature it. Whenever I yelp and my friends and family ask what happened, we have a novel way to hurt ourselves added to my list. Every now and then, we recite the list of ways I've injured myself and laugh till our guts ache. And also I'm not allowed to walk down the basement steps in flip-flops anymore.

Clumsiness isn't the only trait I refused to own. I've spent a lifetime denying or trying to fix all my idiosyncrasies, and I just can't. Instead of fixing them, I need to feature them.

Every year in school, I would start the year off telling my brain that I was going to reinvent myself as the quiet kid. I was determined to be that darling, quiet girl whom everyone liked and never made anyone mad and never said anything the wrong way. By the end of the first class on the first day, I'd end up as the one sitting in the front row with my hand in the air foaming at the mouth. I was never, ever, ever going to be cool. Or quiet. Or demure, whatever the heck that means.

Via Twitter @UnexpectedMel

My dream last night was Jane Austen meets *Inception*. People in knee pants were worrying about a helix & fiddling w/gadgets. My brain is weird.

For so long, I chafed against my personality like a thick, too-tight, itchy wool suit. As I'm letting my personality out for the world to see, I'm feeling less and less tight and itchy and more and more like I'm slipping on a satiny silky robe with plenty of breeziness up in my business end. Life is more comfortable when we're ourselves, and the more you just be you, the more you'll attract two types of people, people like you and people who like you.

> Life is more comfortable when we're
> ourselves, and the more you just be you,
> the more you'll attract two types of people,
> people like you and people who like you.

I don't know about you, but I'm very weird. I possess a potpourri of quirky, bizarre little traits and a penchant for too many colors thrown together. I don't think I'm alone. I think everyone is weird, and a bunch of weirdos makes for a fun playdate.

Let ~~It All~~ Some of It Hang Out

If you're a geek, don't be afraid to go geek. When I start talking about *Buffy the Vampire Slayer*, it sounds like "Get thee to Comic-Con, weirdo." But I've found my people, the ones who like me because of it and the ones who like me in spite of it. The ones who watch it with me and the ones who pray for me.

If you sing and dance around the kitchen with your kids, don't be afraid to bust it out on second base in neutral territory. Maybe start with a few bars of "I Will Survive" and see what happens. Or maybe you feel the urge for some "Livin' on a Prayer." *The Fresh Prince of Bel-Air* theme song is a winner and available to even the tone deafest of mamas. I can't seem to memorize Scripture for all the Awana in the world, but I still know every word to "The Humpty Dance," and don't start it around me or I will finish it. Consider this your parental advisory.

Musical theatre provides a smorgasbord of melodies on which to base a friendship. There are a whole lot of thespian moms out there and you can take the geek out of drama club, but you cannot take the drama out of the mama. From Sondheim to Rogers and Hammerstein, pulling out a little musical theatre on second base is a surefire way to find your fellow Gleeks.

> You can take the geek out of drama club, but you cannot take the drama out of the mama.
>
> ═══════════

On a bike ride with a new friend I started singing the yodeling part from *The Sound of Music*, and she joined in. Immediately, I knew we were meant to be. If you feel like yodeling, do it.

If all else fails, go with Disney. I have this fantasy where all the moms at the park break out into "A Whole New World" and I get to do the "Don't you DARE close your eyes" part. Anybody want to shoot that music video with me?

Personally, I'm a *Sweeney Todd* girl and find myself in the odd predicament of explaining the demon barber of Fleet Street from time to time ... because throat slashing and cannibalism are funny, she says at the new moms' group at church.

The best way to wield your weirdness is with confidence, like a boss. Own it.

If you're a face-painting, sideline-screaming football fan, we're going to want to know that, and we're going to need pictures. Never apologize for grease paint and enthusiasm.

Do you organize your M&M's by color before you eat them? Are you obsessed with *So You Think You Can Dance* and pulled a hammy last week trying to dance alone in your living room? Did you win the March Madness office bracket pool? We need. To know. These awesome things.

If you talk about *Warehouse 13* like it's the greatest show ever created, you will be interesting. Even if the other mom isn't interested in the show, she might be interested in you, because you're excited about something and fun. If you see her start to glaze over, though, take that moment to ask her a question about herself. *Blah blah blah blah blah I'm boring, what do you like to watch and/or read?*

Several years ago, we moved to a new city. I had one child and didn't know anyone. I was terribly lonely for a friend. As an introvert, I found it hard to do anything about that. So I decided, with my normal lack of social skills, to randomly reach out. I accosted a mom of three at the neighborhood park, and invited her to go for a walk. She agreed, and we met early one morning with our little ones, although I got a resentful vibe from her about the meeting time I selected. 7:30 a.m. You see, I had only one child. I didn't realize the exponential amount of work that goes into getting subsequent children out the door. My bad. Anyway, we started walking. The walk ended up taking much longer than we realized. After a couple miles, things started heading south. She became increasingly huffy, and I realized the friendship was a nonstarter. I felt very embarrassed about having made the effort to reach out. Ever after, when I would see her in town, she would pretend not to know me. In retrospect, I don't feel like I did anything wrong, but at the time, I felt like a fool.

I gave up after that, until my husband set me up on a blind date. One day, he came home from the park, telling me he'd met a lady for me. He even got her number. With apprehension, I called her, and we scheduled a playdate at the park. When I arrived, the only person I saw was a strange woman in a large hat, doing side bends and stretches in the middle of the playground. With dismay, I realized this had to be her. I introduced myself, and we started talking. Turns out, she was a breath of fresh air. A little eccentric, wonderfully interesting — just the sort of person who'd be willing to go on a blind date, set up by someone's random husband. We became inseparable. Our girls were the same age, preschoolers, and since we had no other children and no other obligations, we spent most afternoons together, for hours. We'd sit and drink hot tea and talk, or take our girls out to local sights.

After a couple years, we both moved away. I can see she was a gift from God, for that season of our lives. And although we now only correspond by Christmas card, she still holds a treasured place in my heart. — *Amy B.*

Feeding Time

And then there's food weirdness. My favorite people are the ones who pack extra items to share in their picnic lunches. I want to be like them. As their kids are eating The Best Food Ever Because It's Not Ours and my kids start to whine, these prepared Ninja Moms pull out extra baggies of Snack of Gold, saying to their kids, "Can you share our special snack magic with our new friends?" My kids die of happiness and I offer them some old, too squishy grapes in return.

If you want to share your special snack magic, make sure it's allergy-free if you know they have issues, or do that mind-meld thing we moms do with eyebrow raises and miniscule gestures to get on the same page about the possible snack share before presenting it to the masses. (And hey, as an Allergy Mom, I feel weird and awkward and don't want to be all different and high maintenance, but it is what it is. If I say no, I'm sooo not rejecting you, just the food. You totally still get mega points for generosity.)

Everyone has different ways of doing the food thing, so on second base, embracing scenarios where everyone can choose what they need is key. Some moms like to make sure their kids eat all their chicken nuggets before running off to the playground. Others don't really care when the nuggets are eaten as long as they choke them down at some point in the day.

In this realm of motherhood, I sometimes feel the need to conform to what everyone else is doing, and I have to remind myself often that it's okay to be different. As you hang out together and forge relationships, it's great to hear the perspectives of others, but in the end, you're the mother of your unique children, so the decisions are yours.

Be Weird with Me

I love watching my kids make new friends. When they're little, all they know how to do is be themselves. They get silly, make up games, show each other the neat tricks they can do, and tell each other knock-knock jokes. They run full out and jump as high as they can and twirl in circles and try to pick each other up to see who's strongest and biggest.

> **Via Twitter @UnexpectedMel**
>
> Spellcheck hates me. It will not forgive me for typing words like "turdtastic" & "chillsies." Its red underlines are beginning to drive me nuts.

Somewhere along the way, we stop playing with each other. We hide the things that make us unique and we stand quietly together watching our kids have all the fun. But our friendships can be fun too.

Tell me a joke. I'm dying for a good snort laugh. Show me a stupid human trick. Can you make a really weird face that you usually only show your kids? Are you clumsy like I am? Wanna trade stories?

One of my favorite things about getting together with my

dad's side of the family is the storytelling. Growing up, we'd drive to my grandparents' house for a reunion, eat a big meal, delve into a buffet of homemade treats, and sit around my grandparents' living room telling stories. I'd listen to stories from when my parents were growing up, stories of farming and funny relatives and weddings and trips abroad. We'd laugh and laugh, and we'd get louder and louder and louder the harder we laughed and the faster the stories poured out.

Over my lifetime, my aunts' and uncles' and parents' and grandparents' retold stories became old friends, and no matter how many times we heard them, we'd laugh harder and deeper with the familiarity of the memories. After my beloved grandfather's funeral, we went back to the house, back to that living room, and I remember the comfort of hearing the stories once more. The stories that he told have now become part of his legacy. I fell in love with storytelling in my grandparents' living room.

My love for storytelling that started with my family continues with my friendships, and I love nothing better than getting to know another mom over funny stories, from how she met her husband to how she got lost on the way to the park and everything in between. I love stories of faith journeys and stories of squishy diaper explosions.

As our kids play together, be weird with me. Be gloriously and completely yourself. Tell me stories. I want to hear about your new boss and the book you just read that made you mad and how you're questioning God and that time last week when you locked yourself in the bathroom. And tell me about your grandfather and I'll tell you about mine.

Notes

1. *Stand By Me*, directed by Rob Reiner, Columbia Pictures Corporation, 1986.
2. I learned this adage from my favorite professor at Denison University, Cynthia Turnbull. Thanks, Cindi, for teaching me about life and how to cut a gusset.

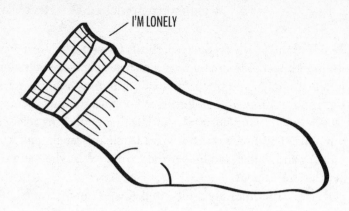

I'M LONELY

|| CHAPTER 14 ||

One Sock Short of a Pair

Guard: "You idiots! These are not them! You've captured their stunt doubles!" From *Spaceballs*[1]

All I do is laundry. It's this constant, never-ending cycle of sorts; treat stains, wash, dry, fold. Do you ever feel like all you do is laundry? Whether you work outside the home, inside the home, on top of the home, or underneath the home, do you just feel like you launder your brains out?

One time on a third-base date I actually helped a friend fold laundry. I highly recommend this practice, if you can get over the uncomfortable reality of touching your friend's husband's boxers. Or make her handle all the skivvies.

This is how laundry day usually goes down in my house. After spending all day schlepping around huge piles of laundry, shoving them into the washer, shoving them into the dryer, and ranting about how we own too many clothes and we're getting rid of half of everything and we are overindulgent, excessive Westerners, I finally sit down to fold everything. I start with the largest items first, because it makes my pile decrease quicker, therefore making me feel like I'm working quicker than I really am.

By the time I'm done with all the shirts, jeans, and jammies, all that remain are the socks. I abhor the socks. They come in all shapes and sizes and it's virtually impossible to locate them all. I find some adhered to the inside of khaki pants and some turned in on themselves and still wet. My husband owns five hundred and twenty-two different styles of black socks, and I feel like I'm going blind trying to distinguish between the three-inch crew socks with the wide ribbing and the five-inch socks with the tiny ribbing.

> **Via Twitter @UnexpectedMel**
> After spending all day washing, drying, and folding clothes, I'm declaring tomorrow "Naked Wednesday," so we can have a day with empty laundry baskets before I start all over.

At the end of the long sock-mating process, I always, ALWAYS, have a few socks left over. They are singles. They have no friends. And I end the laundry day feeling incomplete and a little bit cranky.

Mismatched Moms, Mismatched Kids

When you have a mismatched second-base mom date and you are pondering afterward how it all went down, it can leave you feeling a little like the socks. A perfect mom date is a sock of kids matched with a sock of moms. It's a beauteous, harmonious little matchety match. However, when the sock of kids is fuzzy and warm, but the sock of moms is a stinky mess, or vice versa, what the heck do you do?

When your kids adore each other and can play for hours, but talking to the mom is worse than watching paint dry on a freezing winter day. When your mom friend is your new BFF and you want to grow old with her, but your kids despise each other and make every effort to sabotage your friendship. What do you do when you're one sock short of a pair?

First, let's talk about if it's you and her. As I said before, remember not everyone is going to like you, and you aren't going to like everyone. Please let me absolve you of guilt. It's okay. We don't have to enjoy spending time with everyone. We need to love everyone, to be loving in our actions, to everyone. Humble yourself, serve each other, don't talk badly about another mom, and never intentionally hurt someone. Yes. This is essential. But we don't have to force a relationship when there just isn't one. And frankly, sometimes it's easier to love someone when you're spending less time with her.

In Acts 15:36–41, the Bible shares the story of Paul and Barnabas. "They had such a sharp disagreement that they parted company." Paul took Silas and Barnabas took Mark, and a disagreement launched two missionary teams. Now we'll forgive Paul and Barney for not being moms, but we can still learn something from them. As mothers, we have our own ministry to our children. If we have a relationship with another mom that just isn't flowing, no matter how hard we work at it, rather than gritting our teeth and trying harder, sometimes it's okay to part ways.

If this is you, it's important to remain loving, to seek the best for the other mom, and to avoid speaking negatively about her. If your kids are really close, consider taking turns hosting playdates. She can have a morning off while the kids play at your house, and the next time you can have the morning off. If you remain friendly and positive toward each other, there are ways to keep your children together while you and she experience some necessary apart time.

On the flip side, what if the relationship is missing the other sock? What if you are crazy about the mom but your kids bring out the absolute worst in each other? If you try several times to help your kids get along and it just isn't working out, skip bases and go directly to fourth. You don't have to force your kids to like each other, and if you already know she's amazing, then ask her out for coffee after the kids are in bed one night and enjoy each other without the sounds of shrieking Ringwraiths in the background.

The apostle Paul, who couldn't work it out with Barnabas, still had some pretty awesome things to say about relationships.

> Be completely humble and gentle; be patient, bearing with one another in love. Make every effort to keep the unity of the Spirit through the bond of peace.   EPHESIANS 4:2–3

Make every effort, and then sometimes that means less time for one of the socks.

Notes

1. *Spaceballs*, directed by Mel Brooks, MGM, 1987.

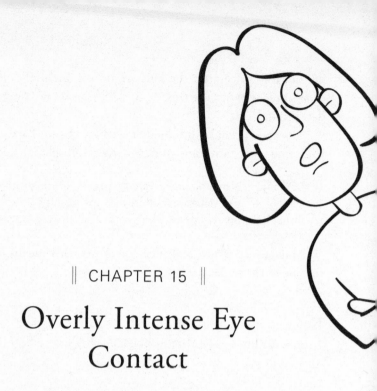

CHAPTER 15

Overly Intense Eye Contact

Dr. Egon Spengler: "Don't cross the streams ... Try to imagine all life as you know it stopping instantaneously and every molecule in your body exploding at the speed of light."

From *Ghostbusters*[1]

We have all been on the other side of someone's eyeballs digging holes into the gooey centers of our brains. It's ... unpleasant. When you run around with a lot of passionate women who spend every day fighting for the very best for their kids and families, fully armed with proton packs, you end up crossing your streams every now and then and can end up with a mess bigger than a giant Stay Puft Marshmallow Man.

We all have opinions and reasons for how we do everything, from staying at home or not, to school and food choices, to diapers and nursing. I spend half my time obsessing about whether or not I'm making the right choices and half my time comparing my choices to those of the moms around me. And honestly, what's so amazing is that we mostly have choice. Although what we do often depends on our calling or our circumstances, our culture allows us to choose whether to stay at home with our kids or not. We aren't fighting to try to get school and food for our kids. Most of us reading this book are choosing from several options in how we live our lives. (I know many of us have not had a choice, have felt trapped or forced or stuck. If this is you, feeling like you didn't get to decide, I just want to recognize that and offer a hug and a nod. I'm seeing you and I'm respecting the heck out of you.)

Homeschool, private school, public school. This year, my son is doing the one on the list I thought I'd *never* do. Ever. But when it came time to make a decision about school, it felt like the best for this year.

And that's all we do as moms, right? We take one year at a time, one decision at a time, and make these weighty choices that impact the lives of our loves. I'll feel pretty good about my choice, pray it up, pray it down, slap my Bible over it, do circles on the couch like my dog, finally lie down in an exhausted heap, and feel at peace. Then I get up, leave the house, talk to another mom who made a different choice and feel completely kerfloofy, go home, collapse all over my husband, make him listen to my pros and cons list all over again, and lather, rinse, repeat.

And sometimes, when I've had a good Holy Spirit enema and have my head on straight, I do the following: when I start to freak out about whether or not I made the right choice, I stop and pray for the kids in the world who don't get to go to school at all.

The same is true for food. Some of us have more options than others, but most of us are not fighting to feed our children. While we feed off of our own insecurities about the choices we make and compare ourselves to each other, other moms in the majority world are struggling to find *any* food for their kids.

And then there's the biggest mom choice of all. In addition to all the hard work of mothering, what about working an additional job, whether it's in an office or on a computer in your kitchen?

Did your butt just clench up a bit? I'm clenching as I try to figure out the right words to type. We desperately need to learn a language of respect for all mothers in the ways they juggle careers and the hard work of having a family.

Link Arms and Pray

Instead of disagreeing with each other about our parenting choices, what if we celebrated that we have choice? What if we used our freedom to stop fighting each other and start fighting extreme poverty together? Let's all aim our proton packs at poverty and disease. (I realize some of you may be giving me overly intense eye contact about my movie references right now. That's fair.) Let's fight human trafficking. Let's fight for the kids who don't have families. Let's fight anything but each other when we have so much work to do in the world.

> Let's fight anything but each other when we
> have so much work to do in the world.

Right now, I want you to stop and pray for the kids who need school and food and families and freedom. For the ones who don't have mamas to fight for them. Pray for the mamas who are wringing their hands in desperation for the next meal to feed their babies. Pray for the kids spending all day looking for water rather than learning how to read.

I'm moderately, ravenously passionate about this.

I promise I'm still blinking. I'm not making overly intense eye contact as you read this. I'm being cool.

So, in a world that likes division and categories, that sections us into the homeschoolers and the public schoolers, the breast-feeders and the bottle feeders, the "working moms" and the "stay-at-home moms" (I'm using quote marks sarcastically here, because do any of us think those categories are sufficient?), how do we link arms? It's all well and good to preach about how we can change the world, but how do we navigate a simple second-base date, with all of its intricacies of differing thoughts and opinions and experiences?

I think the answer is listening to each other. When navigating different needs or preferences, I try to listen well, to be a learner. When someone does something differently than I do, whether by choice or necessity, I want to ask good questions and listen. Really listen.

When we catch ourselves sliding into the clutches of comparison or feel judgment creeping up the back of our throats, I want us to remember who the enemy is. It isn't the mom over there who looks like she has it all together and seems confident in her choices. It isn't her. The enemy is the one who is prowling around the world stealing light from the eyes of children. It's empty bellies and empty souls and it's poverty ripping babies away from their mamas.

All our fighting about our choices ... it's a distraction to keep us from seeing the real issues. And when we link arms together and choose friendship over argument, we can change the world.

> Listen, don't get trapped in brainless debates; avoid competition over family trees or pedigrees; stay away from fights and disagreements over the law. They are a waste of your time.
>
> TITUS 3:9 (*VOICE*)

Notes

1. *Ghostbusters*, directed by Ivan Reitman, Columbia Pictures, 1984.

Part 3
THIRD BASE

CHAPTER 16

It's About to Get Real

Rachel: "Oh, honey. Don't get up. What do you need?"

Phoebe: "Oh, no. Oh, nothing."

Rachel: "Come on. I am here to take care of you. What do you need? Anything."

Phoebe: "Okay, I have a wedgie."

Rachel: "Okay, that is all you."

From *Friends*[1]

So you've made it to third base. It's about to get real. Up in here. Up. In. Here. Third base is not for people who pretend they have it all together. Even if you can manage a decent façade for a couple of hours, on third base, your kids will out you before you can say, "Welcome to my home." On third, your kids are playing on home field, which means they'll act like they do at home, which means your friend will see how your kids actually behave and how you handle or don't handle it. Yeah.

If that doesn't scare the crapstick out of you, let me describe a recent third-base date I had. Everyone's behavior was actually not too horrific. We were doing well. And then.

My friend's three-year-old took a dump in the upstairs bathroom and used the entire roll of toilet paper. As she walked out, eschewing the apparently optional hand-washing idea, I walked in to a rapidly rising toilet of man-sized floaters. I surveyed the scene and did what any excellent hostess would do. I walked right out. I did. I just pretended like I had no idea that was going down, or actually not going down, which was the problem.

I heard my own three-year-old screaming from the downstairs bathroom, and as I entered that hot mess, my nostrils promptly lost all nose hair, burnt right off from the toxic stench of my daughter's turdly disaster. As I bent over to wipe her, she apologized, "I'm sorry, Mommy." I didn't understand this and assured her that poop is normal and to poop in the potty is fabulous and no apology needed. And then I helped her off the potty.

Prior to my entering the scene, she had used her butt as a paintbrush, a paintbutt if you will, to smear feces from the base of the potty up the side, around the seat, on her undies, shorts, and sparkly light-up shoes. All I could get out was, *"How!?!?"* in a strained, desperate voice. While she washed her hands, I peeled the undies and shorts off and threw them in the trash, because, just, whatever, I couldn't handle it with my friend right upstairs sitting on my couch and who knows if she'd discovered the clogged toilet yet.

Via Facebook @UnexpectedMel

Things I never thought I'd have to say: Evie, toilet paper is for wiping. We do not eat it. We do not rub it on our face. We do not get it wet and paper mâché the bathroom floor. My sermon was well-received.

I cleaned the toilet, the tile, and the grout, then hoisted Poopie Monster up the stairs and into a quick bath, because stuff was in places that wasn't coming off without soaking.

New outfit, drain the tub, the obligatory forty-eight rounds of hand washing, and I was back on the couch to resume talking with my friend about what a typical day looks like for us. Did I mention that she's from out of town and I never see her so she has no basis for what my typical day looks like and might think that I spend every day covered in dookie?

And then I see my husband come out of the clogged bathroom. Bless his heart. He'd handled it and my friend was none the wiser. Until now, if she's reading this book.

After she and her gang left, another friend came over with her gaggle of children, and at this point, you might be wondering what kind of mom-dating Casanova I am. What can I say, my animal magnetism and toilet seats draw them in, ladies. You know you want some.

My friend asked where the bathroom was, and when she came back, let me know that she almost sat in poop and had to clean off the seat. Because apparently my child number two (pun intended) took a dump in between rocking playdates and somehow smeared it on the seat, or maybe Clogger Girl left some remnants. I'm not sure. The point is, it's impossible to die of embarrassment because I tried right then and it didn't work.

Via Facebook @UnexpectedMel

Double out-of-towner mom dates today. I'm pulling out all the stops. I showered, have on actual clothes, am wearing shoes, and brushed my teeth. I know. Dude. This is for real.

The next day, as I walked upstairs, I discovered that our banister was also covered in dried poo.

And this is third base. Not every date is this disgusting and most people don't have moms coming in and out of their houses like they're operating a coffeepot at Grand Central Station, but for sure, third base, it's real life, which for us, apparently means gross.

Notes

1. "The One with Ross's Wedding: Part 1," *Friends*, National Broadcasting Company, aired May 7, 1998.

|| CHAPTER 17 ||

The Superpower of Initiating

The Shoveller: "Lucille, God gave me a gift. I shovel well. I shovel very well."

Lucille: "Honey, you shovel better than any man I've ever known, but that does not make you a superhero."

From *Mystery Men*[1]

A few years ago, I took my son to a sporty night for the high school kids at church. My husband and I have served as youth leaders since these teens entered sixth grade, and one summer in the Georgia heat, we all decided it was a great idea to meet once a week and do sporty things.

I can't even remember what sport, which says all you need to know about my athletic ability. Maybe soccer or ultimate Frisbee. That's a thing, right? Anyway, I took Elliott to the nearby park while my husband kicked and/or threw athletic paraphernalia. There I saw Donna, also at the park with her son, the same age as mine. We were "hi/bye" church lobby acquaintances. She actually is quite sporty, but happened to be nine months pregnant, which brought her down to my sad level of activity.

As the boys played, we talked, and I realized what an answer to prayer she was. My sweet Rose had just moved away, and I had a sucking wound in my chest. I was lonely. I'd asked God for a new friend, and he answered with Donna.

I'm not saying this direct path would work for everyone, but I texted Donna later exactly that. Yeah, reading it on the page as I type this, hearing that you're an answer to prayer would not work on everyone and could make some people freak out a bit. But thankfully for me, Donna texted me back and we trotted to second base, meeting weekly at the local library with our boys for story time, then on to third base with weekly playdates at my cluttered house.

The Pleasure of Being Pursued

Freaky pickup lines notwithstanding, people like being pursued. Think about how you felt when your husband or boyfriend pursued you. Desirable. Wanted. Valued. Needed. Lovely. Worthy.

> Freaky pickup lines notwithstanding,
> people like being pursued.
> =============

If you regularly ask people to do things, you possess a superpower that not everyone has. The ability to initiate is a gift. It takes thick skin and motivation. If you're an initiator, whether you know it or not, people appreciate you and need you around. We are drawn to those women who are always getting people together, organizing activities, and planning playdates. If you're naturally gifted at introducing people, pulling people together, and inviting people to do things, don't stop. We need you.

I hear a lot of frustration from initiators who feel like they are always the ones making the call and reaching out. I've felt that way from time to time. The best friendships I have are the ones where we share the initiating, where we take turns. And that doesn't mean back and forth like clockwork. During different seasons, one person might take the lead. If your friend has just had a baby, this might be your opportunity to do the inviting and planning and not expect anything in return. And if you have to take care of your mom after her surgery, then your friend might assume responsibility for calling and checking in on you.

So often the expectations we put on each other are the downfall of our relationships. I invite someone for a playdate. I expect them to call and invite me the next time. They don't. I feel hurt, I start to question if they even like me, and I let my insecurities fester until my thoughts about my friend are completely negative. Maybe she's been battling a flu bug that's worming its way through all her kids. Maybe she's freaking out about her own junk and is afraid to call me. Maybe there are a thousand possibilities and if I just pick up the phone and invite her out again, we'll have a great time and who cares whose idea it is?

> So often the expectations we put on each other
> are the downfall of our relationships.

Initiate without Resentment

As initiators, the important thing is to do it without resentment. If your friend always wants to come to your house but never invites you to hers, you can feel resentment. If she takes forever to text you back, resentment. If you feel close enough to her to tell her how you feel, let her know in a gentle, easygoing, non-accusatory way that you'd love for her to pick the day and activity next time. If you value your time with her and she just isn't the initiating type, you have to either let the resentment go and just enjoy hanging out, or lose that friendship. When you start to feel resentment sneak in, replace it with thankfulness and appreciation. What do you like about this mama? Remind yourself of why you enjoy her company in the first place. Above all, live fester-free.

Go Ahead and Annoy

Sometimes we're afraid to ask a mama out because we don't want to be annoying. I say, don't be afraid to be annoying. Frankly, I don't find it annoying when another mom wants to hang out with me. Even if it doesn't work with our schedule this time, it's never annoying. I am always playing "tag" with several friends who are just busy and juggling a lot and we text and message and text and message and we just keep trying until we're eyeball to eyeball over a cup of coffee. There

> **Via Twitter @UnexpectedMel**
>
> "Mom, why do I have to get dressed? You're still in YOUR jammies." Touché, punk.

are some friends who are just tough to nail down. When you take two different families, mama schedules, and the schedules of a bajillion kids, you end up with this crazy-metamorphosis-of-a-delicate-balance-of-a-house-of-cards schedule. All it takes is one fever, a pile of vomit, or a rained-out soccer practice to make the whole thing collapse and your mom date goes kaput. Persevere. Start texting for the next attempt.

The Last-Minute Date

Of course, you can go the other way too, and try the drive-by mom date, the last-minute, "Hey wanna come over in five minutes; no you don't have to shower I haven't even brushed my teeth today" kind of tryst. Sometimes the busier I am, the easier the last-minute date is. When my schedule is tight, I can't shove one more thing in it, but if I have an unexpected hour, I'll text a friend and go for it. River and I constantly struggle to find time together, like somehow our kids and their schedules are conspiring to keep us apart. Last week, she called and asked me to lunch and I actually had an hour, and we grabbed fast food and talked each other's brains out before car pool pickup at preschool. I never, ever would've put that time slot on my calendar, because I'm normally not available then, but we both just ended up with a free hour. Bown-chicka-bown-owwnn.

Desperation. Survival. When I think back on the stage of life that found me in a new city where I knew no one and I had thirteen-month-old twin girls, these are the two words that come to mind.

Now I know people who might find the "new town, no friend" situation as a challenge or even exciting, but for this introverted mama, it was a scary, helpless place to be. I am that girl who looks enviously around at all the tight-knit girl friendships and immediately thinks two things: they aren't looking for another friend and they wouldn't like me anyway. Insecure, are we? When it comes to girlfriends, the answer is a resounding YES! I have notoriously stunk at making lasting, nonthreatening, genuine girl relationships. Add in the fact that I'm not a super social person and you have me: that awkward new-girl type whom everyone assumes "has it all together" but who really is just waiting to be invited along to the playdate/lunch/book club/walking/crafting (fill in the blank) group. BUT here is a significant truth I have learned: few women do the pursuing.

I finally put on my big girl pants during those desperate early months of my new town/no friends/twin babies predicament. I essentially got "fixed up" with a girl who was also new to the area and who just happened to have twin boys two months younger than my girls. My desperation caused me to act uncharacteristically and I pursued this friendship and threw caution to the wind. What I found was another desperate twin-mama who needed me as much as I needed her. I did not have to pretend with her. I was real with her and in turn she was real with me. It was not unusual to see us at a park with our four crazies running wild while we were still in our PJ's with naked faces! We were just happy to see the outside of our houses. We talked, exchanged disciplining tricks (many of which were epic fails), cried some, and wondered together what just one kid would have been like. We even, on occasion, were brave enough to venture outside of our reclusive world together and were often stopped and asked if those four blond babies were quads. Thank heavens, no! She and I made countless PB&Js together and would turn a blind eye to the gooey sticky mess covering our kitchen floors. We literally, more than once, proved the verse true that says two are better than one. — *Carolyn M.*

Notes

1. *Mystery Men*, directed by Kinka Usher, Universal Pictures, 1999.

‖ CHAPTER 18 ‖

Navigating Your Child's Social Awkwardness

Obi-Wan Kenobi: "Your clones are very impressive. You must be very proud."

From *Star Wars: Episode II—Attack of the Clones*[1]

In one hour, your doorbell is going to ring, and that mom you've been casually seeing is going to walk across the threshold into your world. You're freaking out.

Will she smell the faint odor of salmon that you've been trying to get out of your oven for three days? Will your dog greet her with his usual happy spritz of urine? Will your kids beat her kids to a pulp when they try to take apart the Lego X-wing starfighter spaceship? Should you make a pot of coffee—oh crap you don't have creamer. Don't most women like creamer? You drink yours black like an eighty-year-old man, but then you're not really a girl and don't know how to have these relationships and why are you bothering and what are you going to talk about for two hours?

These are some of the thoughts that have flitted through my brain pre-mom date. Breathe. It's gonna be awesome.

Playdate Proofing Your Home

First, let's talk about playdate proofing your home. This is like child proofing the first time, only deeper, because you're about to host kids who don't know your rules.

If your friend has a crawler and you haven't had one of those in a while, pay attention to the pile of windpipe-shaped marbles hanging out on the floor and the dog bowl just waiting to be sampled. If you want your friend to be able to relax and actually sit down for a bit, find some age-appropriate toys or Tupperware from the kitchen for the toddler to play with near where you're sitting.

I have a conversation with my kids ahead of time and explain who's coming and what's going to go down. Let them put away their uber most favoritist toy that they just spent a month building in their little OCD world. It's not worth the heartache and insanity that will ensue if something happens to it.

Talk to your kids about sharing, role-play what it looks like to share, and prepare them for other kids touching their stuff. Emphasize that their friends won't take anything home, but that they'll just play for a little while. Encourage your kids to pick out toys that they think their friends will like and help them brainstorm ideas for fun.

> **Via Twitter @UnexpectedMel**
>
> During my afternoon chess match with Elliott . . .
>
> Me: It's your turn; where are you going?
>
> El: Over here. I have to toot.
>
> Me: Uh . . . that's really considerate.

My house usually smells like a mixture of whatever the dog just did and whatever the kids just did, so I have a little cinnamon-smelling thing that makes me feel better about our combined stenches.

Don't bother putting on airs, because your kids or your pets will out you as the faker you are. I remember fondly the day I invited a group of moms over and tried to be slightly fancy. I cleaned and made coffee and did that thing where you set the mugs out next to the coffeepot and put baked goods on trays. Suzy Homemaker, that was me. I arranged chairs in a circle and we chatted as we nibbled muffins. We were dainty and well-mannered. A total act, on my part, but I was Pulling It Off.

> Don't bother putting on airs, because your kids or your pets will out you as the faker you are.

As the last mom left and I went to turn off the coffeepot, my toe kicked something on the floor.

It was a turd. It was a TURD. My dog had dropped a deuce right by the coffeepot at some point during the morning and no one had said anything. And it was in a high-traffic area. Every person there must've walked right up to it as they poured their coffee. Thanks, Spike. Welcome to my turdtastic home.

Someone Else's House

My kids go one of two ways when I take them to someone else's house. Sometimes they're so excited to play with someone else's toys that they are happy and sweet and I try to just go with it and stay out of their way. Usually on days like these, the kids on their home court are the ones falling apart because they have to share and they don't like my stinky ol' kids touching their Elmo and blocks.

And then there are the days when my kids are so rude and awful that I just want to slink back to my van and never leave the house again. While my daughter is bossing everyone around and declaring herself Supreme Queentessa of the Empire of the Planet and forcing her little minions to do her bidding, my son is draping himself over the armchair where I'm sitting, whining in a loud voice, "I'm so BORED. This is BORING. They don't have any good toys and everyone here is a baby."

Yeah. Yeah. Just, yeah. These are the days when I wonder how we have any friends.

So when we're entering third-base territory, things can get a little messy and your kids will embarrass you. They will. Before we go over to someone's house, I explain the whole situation to my kids. Here's where we're going, here's what you're going to get to do, here are the unknowns, here's what's going to happen to you if you choose to behave inappropriately, and here's what you get if you make good choices.

Oh yeah, bribe them. You heard me. One piece of gum will turn my girl into a little angel and when I see the horns growing back I just mouth "gum" and she adjusts. For my son, his precious video game time on the weekend is the highlight of his week (so sad — feel free to judge us), and one mention of losing it will usually bump him back from the edge.

If your kids are being complete insanazoids and you feel like you need to offer some excuse besides just, "Um, yeah, sometimes they're awful," here's a handy list of excuses:

She needs a nap.
She hasn't been sleeping well.
He's teething.
His six-year molars are coming in.
He had a rough day at school.
Growth spurt.
Allergies.
Pet hamster just died.
Pediatric carpal tunnel syndrome.
When she was born, the waiting room at the hospital was showing *The View* and now she can't quit arguing.
New footie jammies kept him up all night.

As moms, we have our own bizarre quirks and total weirdness, but that's nothing compared to the social awkwardness of our children. Our years of experience have fine-tuned our inner monsters to where we can say things like "Oh no, you take the last scone. It's yours. I don't need it. I want you to have it." Sure. Our children, young babes that they are, have not gone through the seasoning of years of relationships and say things like "I want that! I want it now! Mine! Mine! Mine!" or even more disturbing, they act like the munchkins who came to my house last year.

I'd made the gluten-free, dairy-free banana muffins that my kids love, and this was the first indicator that we've lost our ability to be able to tell if something is truly yummy to the rest of the world. These kids took one bite of my awesome muffin made of bean flour held together by xanthan gum and mushy bananas and they exclaimed, "I don't like this! It's gross!"

We moms spend our entire lives huddled over hot stoves, crouched in crowded pantries, and lost in the dark mires of our refrigerators. I'm embarrassed that I have to ask my kids why they need to eat three square meals a day. Why do they insist on a snack every time I sit down? Why aren't they eating what I prepared? Why is half of it on the floor? Why am I throwing out most of what's left on their plates? Don't they know that there are starving children in Africa? Why are we having macaroni and cheese for the third time this week? And maybe most humbling of all — why am I the one eating the congealed leftovers that are strewn across the table? Why? Why? Why? I remember the first time my friend invited me over for hot soup and homemade bread. She didn't ask me to bring anything. I found real utensils and a napkin at my place setting. Yes, my place setting! We sat at the table and savored every bite. I'm not even talking about the food. Of course it was delicious, but it was the conversation that warmed my soul that day. And it was the beginning of a beautiful relationship. — *Chantel A.*

All Children Misbehave

There are three main categories to the social awkwardness of our children. Tattling, whining, and violence. When we smoosh our kids together and make them try to be friends, any or all of these things tend to happen. If you want to survive third base, beeee cooooollllll. Seriously, we all need to take a chillsies about it. All children misbehave. All moms want them not to misbehave. When it comes to teaching our kids to get along, we're going to have different styles, and if we value the friendship, we have to give each other a ton of grace in this area.

Since my children haven't had time to manifest into axe murderers, I might be the last person who needs to give parenting advice. You never know if what I'm doing will pan out. But, well, if you're desperate, here are my own general guidelines for playdate decorum.

Tattling

If your child tattles, see if it's something he can solve on his own before you get involved. If he's tattling because someone is hurting him or breaking things, then get in there and stop the destruction, but whenever possible, urge the kids to work it out directly between each other. You're there as a guide, not as a go-between. I want my kids to learn how to work through issues in a direct method, not use me as a mediator.

Speaking of working through issues directly, my son recently had to experience some consequences for his behavior at a playdate. At the end of the day, he refused to help his friend clean up the toys. His friend rightfully got mad at him, and the next time they saw each other, the boy refused to talk to him. I had a talk about the importance of cleaning up the messes we make, both figuratively and metaphorically. The next time we got together, Elliott apologized to his friend, and every time we have playdates and he doesn't want to clean up, I remind him how it felt when his friend got mad at him. I was able to guide him, but I left him to clean up his own relational mess. The older my kids get, the more I can do this.

Whining

Mommy doesn't understand whining. I just try to ignore everything that sounds whiny. *Have a do over.* If my kid is whining about how there's nothing to do or she doesn't want to play here, I try to offer a couple of suggestions for activities, then put it back on her. *Here's the toy closet. Check out these pirate ship Legos. This is your reality for the next hour, so find something to do, play with your friend, and use your imagination. Mommy's playing with her friend, and you play with yours. We're all here to play with our friends.*

> **Via Twitter @UnexpectedMel**
>
> My kids are whining so much that I just made them clean bathrooms. I expect them to start singing songs from *Annie* any second.

And then there was that time the whining was so colossal we had to leave a birthday party early and everyone watched as I carried his flailing body out to the car. #thestruggleisreal

Violence

If her child hurts your child, that does not make him a psychopath, or her a terrible mom. Kids test boundaries and make mistakes. Help your child forgive the one who hurt him. If it keeps happening and the other mom doesn't seem proactive in wrangling her child, then you may need to find solutions with her or the playdates and bullying may need to stop. We hope it doesn't get to that, but it might.

> **Via Twitter @UnexpectedMel**
>
> My kids are screaming at each other "I'M NOT FIGHTING!" Hilarious. #smh

If your child hurts her child, use the moment to teach your child to apologize. I usually force my kid to hug it out and ask questions like, "How can you make her feel better? What do you say? What do you do when you accidentally or on purpose hurt someone?"

If it's clearly an "on purpose" infraction and your child seems completely unrepentant and just itching to get another piece of that kid as soon as your back is turned, go with a time-out. Get your kid away from hers. It gives your kid a few minutes to get it together and gives you a few minutes to figure out what the heck to do. Once back in the game, if your child goes for broke, try making her sit next to you. If that doesn't work, just go home and try again some other time.

No matter how well my kids behave themselves, they're still going to have to deal with the consequences of being around their socially awkward mama. They can work through their own issues, use their imaginations, and refrain from violence until the *Enterprise* comes home, but Mom's still going to sing show tunes and do her Yoda impression. Awkward I am. Embarrass them I will.

Notes

1. *Star Wars: Episode II—Attack of the Clones*, directed by George Lucas, Lucasfilm, 2002.

|| CHAPTER 19 ||

Dating (When You're) a "Working Mom"

Bob Porter: "Looks like you've been missing a lot of work lately."
Peter Gibbons: "I wouldn't say I've been missing it, Bob."
From *Office Space*[1]

You've met at your child's Saturday morning baseball game or evening hip-hop class. You've enjoyed hanging out in a group setting. Now you want to take the relationship further, but when on earth do you fit that into your already busy life? Beyond the weird and awkward, often one of the biggest hurdles for mom dating is scheduling, and those of you who work outside the home know this challenge intimately. When it feels like all the other mamas are getting together without you, what's a working mom* to do (AKA Mom-Who-Goes-to-a-Job-Site-or-Office, or MWGTAJSOO)?

(*We all work, and many of us have shuffled in and out of stay-at-home, go-to-work, and work-from-home. A lot of us have done both, waffle between the two, and defy category. I'm all for defying category. These arbitrary titles and sides are insufficient. There is one team, and we are all on it. Go, team, go. Booty pat. In this chapter, I want us to talk about dating and the challenges and beauty of friendships with moms who go to offices or job sites every day and therefore cannot do daytime playdates.)

How to Date When You Are a Working Mom

So you're a mom with two employers, your children and your company. Maybe your kids have reached school age and you're heading back to work or maybe you never left. Whatever the case, working a job and providing for your family is awesome. Sometimes you can feel stretched between family and career, and now I'm asking you to try to spend time with friends too? Do you need to call me names? Insert name-calling here_____. (If you run out of room, feel free to use the margins, unless you borrowed this book from your friend.)

So, MWGTAJSOO, how do you squeeze friends into an already squozen schedule? First, take a realistic look at your week and figure out when you're available. Listen, you do not have to juggle mom dates all week. But are there a couple of spots in a month where you could invite a friend to do something or maybe say yes to a mom who's been eyeballing you?

Sometimes when you're at work, the office kind of becomes the first- and second-base neutral territory where you get to know each other casually in the break room or walking to the subway. If you like each other and feel a connection, third base is where you might bring in the kids and actually schedule something after work or on the weekend. If you commute and live on opposite sides of the city, your kids may rarely meet. And that's okay.

Once you've pinpointed a third-basey friend, how do you take the relationship deeper? If both of you are seeking spiritual growth, you could invite her to get together once a week to pray or discuss a book together. A lot of Bible studies for moms happen in the morning during the week. This leaves you, MWGTAJSOO, with little opportunity to pray and do all the Bible studies available to your stay-at-home counterparts. If you attend a church with a moms' group that meets at night, great. If not, why not make your own with your friend? If you're tired, live far away, or smell and don't feel like showering, you can do this over the phone.

If you or some of your crew are going back to work now that the kids are older, you might have to start scheduling. The days of last-minute drop-ins during the week may fizzle, but now you're entering the precious territory of prioritizing time together. Don't take it for granted that you'll bump into each other. Plan it ahead of time. Part of the joy of the date is the very anticipation that it's coming soon. You'll still talk about your kids, but now you'll also talk about your jobs. On the flip side, don't be afraid to call her to meet for dinner as you're walking out of the office. You never know if she's craving chips and salsa too.

> Don't take it for granted that you'll bump
> into each other. Plan it ahead of time.

How to Date a Working Mom

Hi, Stay-At-Home Mom (AKA Always-on-the-Go-Go-and-Never-Stays-at-Home, or AOTGGANSAH). If you find yourself in deep like with your air traffic controller neighbor or ophthalmologist friend at church or teller at the bank, how do you develop the relationship when your schedules are completely different? She's pulling in the driveway right when you've hit the witching hour and you're both drained of all your life force. How can this relationship work?

I have a few ideas.

Invite her over for dinner. It's hard coming home from work and switching from work mode to home mode and trying to give hugs, talk homework, and figure out what to feed everybody. Sometimes it's nice to just show up to a meal that's ready. Don't do fancy. Think Crock-Pot. The important thing is full bellies and time together. If you don't feel like cooking, suggest a kid-friendly restaurant where you can meet or order takeout. I like this on a Friday night, because bedtimes aren't an issue, so the kids can stay up a little later than usual and everyone's glad it's the weekend. Order pizza and scoop ice cream out of a big tub.

If she's exhausted after work and out of words and just wanting jammies and the couch, what about lunch or the park after church on Sunday? You're already out, wearing reasonably clean clothes. What's one more hour of interacting with people?

Invite her over for coffee and donuts on Saturday morning or meet somewhere. She's been in work clothes all week, so make it sweat pants-only. Please. Like I even have to tell you that.

When you get together, ask her about her job, what she loves about it, her favorite parts, her boss. Show interest in this big part of her life. Find out what made her choose this career, what she's learned over the years. Don't ask her how she can leave her kids or say that you could never leave your kids. Just don't. You know this, AOTGGANSAH. You would never.

One Size Definitely Doesn't Fit All

I'm very aware that the way I date moms may not work for everyone and every schedule. The flexibility of your work schedule, including kids, employers, and which balls in the air are flying where, can dictate your availability for mom dating. As a work-from-home mom (AKA Works-in-Jammies-with-Children-Banging-on-the-Door, or WIJWCBOTD), I have a bit of flexibility with mom dates, because while I generally try to do my non-kid work while the munchkins are at school, I often can shift things around and snag some time with a friend. My mom dates are scattered all over the calendar, from morning dates to evening dates after the kids are in bed.

I have a friend named Lindsey who's a lawyer. I met her through Children's HopeChest, and we only knew each other through phone calls and tweeting each other. Clearly, I skip around on my own mom dating rules, because the first time we got together was when we both road-tripped our families and met in Memphis for a weekend. Just because. What base is that?!? I don't even know! Like, around the bases, back in the locker room, sharing a bag of peanuts.

When I started writing this book, I asked my hilarious friend what it's like trying to develop momlationships as a mother who works outside her home and shows up at an office every day. Here's what she has to say about mom dating.

I hate the term "working mom." No matter what comes before your name, if the word "mom" in any way defines you, you work. And you work hard. I've heard several alternate forms of descriptions for women who have paycheck-acquiring jobs, but they all seem to suck too. My personal, self-described title for what I do is "the $100,000 law school loan payoff plan." There. I typed it out loud. My law school education cost me six figures. My mama obviously raised a fool. And this fool came to my marriage with a higher monthly debt obligation than my hubby's first house payment. So I pack a briefcase every day.

Here are my top ten personal disclaimers on dating moms who bring home a paycheck.

1. I am more terrified of you than you will ever be of me. I am judged every day for "making the decision to work outside the home," and therefore I am more likely to be planning an escape attempt out of our relationship, even before it begins. If you are a SAHM, the probability of this occurring increases 1000%. I believe that you are judging me, even when you are not, and I cannot carry anyone else's opinion of me about my parenting choices. The "mommy wars" can kiss it. I have car pool.

2. Please address all questions about my paycheck-bringing activities in a way you would want to be asked about your daily activities. Every mom has her own version of mom guilt.

Mine leaves me in tears after dropping off at day care and simultaneously smiling like an idiot while I drive to the office because for fifteen minutes no one is saying my name. This manic, love-hate relationship with "working" is why God created therapists.

3. I am a horrible match for moms who can only tolerate one friend at a time. This is not true of all out-of-the-house moms, but for me, I am better if our dating life is more like Lionel Richie's "Easy Like Sunday Morning" and not some version of a creepy 1980s love song. The pressure of anyone relying on me for huge things in the beginning makes me want to bolt. See #1.

4. Impromptu dates are common and occur often. Do not be offended if sporadic texts for a meet-up are sent hours or minutes in advance. I am not offended at rejection, even if it is several times in a row. I roll with flexibility.

5. Changing shoes, removing jewelry, and switching bras is considered a complete wardrobe change. If I tell you I've got to run home and change and you notice nothing different, look at my feet. A pencil skirt and flip-flops is a completely different feel than a pencil skirt and heels. Also, entire changes of clothes for each member of my family can be found in the back of my car, along with a second makeup bag, hair care and every wrinkle releaser, stain remover, cloth wipe, baby wipe, and deodorant on the market. Survival techniques.

6. Do not be offended if during a date, especially in the beginning, my phone, tablet, etc. are vibrating, ringing, and singing simultaneously and I am trying to gnaw my fingers off to keep from reaching them. It's not rude. It's self-preservation.

7. Do not be afraid to fight your date's flux between complete micromanaging ease and sheer laziness. Depending on the day, I feel the need to have an opinion over everything or I have exerted everything I have at the office and will have to

leave every detail of our date to you.

8. Please reserve all comments about parenting decisions until your opinion has been solicited. Remember that we are both being judged for our choices. Whether by society, our mothers, our mother-in-laws, our bosses, someone, somewhere is telling us we suck at our job. And I've probably told myself that already fifteen times today.

9. There is nothing magical about having an office. Remove any ideas of grandeur from your mind. Think of it as another place where everyone knows your name and continues to repeat it so often you think you're amongst your own toddlers. Board meetings, entertaining clients, work trips away from home, and late nights at the office can all be substituted by homeschooling, coloring, field trips, and late-night feedings. We're all doing things every day, but because what you and I do may differ, sometimes we believe the lie that she's got it better. Nope. She's just dealing with a different group of toddlers.

10. Wine, coffee, and chocolate cover a multitude of bad days. Sometimes showing up with a bottle of red and a bag of M&M's is the perfect love language. But isn't that the trademark of dating moms anyway, just showing up?

— *Lindsey Andrews*

Well, after all this talk about the complexities of playdates and working, who needs a hug? I know I do.

Notes

1. *Office Space*, directed by Mike Judge, Twentieth Century Fox, 1999.

CHAPTER 20

The Anatomy of a Full-Frontal Hug

Principal Flutie: "We all need help with our feelings.
Otherwise we bottle them up, and before you know it,
powerful laxatives are involved ... I'm always here if you
need a hug, but not a real hug! Because there's no touching.
This school is sensitive to wrong touching."

From *Buffy the Vampire Slayer*[1]

Okay, ladies, let's break this thing on down. Full-frontal hugging. Like with handshaking, the lead-in, duration, pressure, and dismount are all important.

So you think you're ready for hugging. If you're like me, that happens fast. Some of you need a longer warm-up time or you could go an entire lifetime hug-free, but you choose to take pity on those of us who need a good boob mash-up to survive.

It's third base, you're on home field, or her home field. Do you crack one off on the way in or wait for when you leave?

It's up to you. Personal preference. If you're unsure, you can go for a side-hug on the way in, or a light frontal with zero torso contact. You'll be carrying diaper bags, car seats, or Druscilla's soy-free, vegan snacks in a baggie, so your hands are full and an awkward pull in and release might be all that's necessary.

If I'm really going for it and can't contain my ardor, I'll drop all my stuff right there in the entryway to your house and pull it on in for a full-on, mammogram-esque, booby mash-up. If you're lucky, I won't hold it too long.

> If I'm really going for it and can't contain my ardor, I'll drop all my stuff right there in the entryway to your house and pull it on in for a full-on, mammogram-esque, booby mash-up. If you're lucky, I won't hold it too long.

———

Let's talk about duration. You'll sense from the other person what her limit is. I can go all day with a good hug, so I usually feel out how tense and awkward the other person is and release as needed. When they pull away a bit to try to talk to you, you'll know they can't take it much longer.

If you're on the receiving end and need it to end so you can breathe, try a squeeze off, a little squeeze then release. The other mom gets a deeper hug, and you get freedom on the other side of it.

You may be asking, what do I do with my arms? Great question. For a mom-to-mom hug, you're going to want one arm on top, one on bottom. Anything else will feel like you're at a middle school dance, in which case there'd better be some "Unchained Melody," Boys II Men, and swaying from side to side. Personally, I'm a left leaner on a hug. I lean left, left arm goes under the mom date's right arm, right arm goes on top of her left arm, boobs together, and mash. Chin over the shoulder, smile, and squeeze, turning your head to the side to breathe sweet nothings of mom solidarity into her right ear. Inhale, exhale, hug it out.

If you aren't ready at the beginning of the date, by the end you may need one after you've bonded over how psycho each other's kids are.

I recently attended a conference where I was able to read an excerpt from this book, and when you write about boob mash-ups and invite women to bring it on in, you're going to get what you asked for. While other women at the conference were having deeply spiritual moments together with tears and tissues and emotion, I was having women come up to full-frontal me on the elevator, waiting in line for lunch, and I even had a woman chest bump me with her boobs. Not even a hug, just a booby pound-it. I loved everything about these new friends, and it made me really glad I'd gone bra shopping right before the event.

Every week, my husband and I go out for a date before our married couples' group gets together. We had some time between gluten-free pizza and driving to our friends' house, so I said I wanted to duck into a store for a new bra. Take breastfeeding, throw in a little age and a little gravity, and you have the girls floundering on my chest not really sure where they're supposed to be. I needed a bra that would slide them in their place.

I suggested that Alex hang out in the car and wait for me, but he was like, "Are you kidding me? Bra shopping? I'm going in the dressing room with you, yeah baby yeah." I really don't think he knew what he was getting into, bless his little XY heart.

We walked in and were greeted by a lovely saleswoman. She asked what size I was. I wasn't sure anymore, again because of all the floundering. Now. Never go into a bra store and tell them you don't know your size unless you're ready to be wo-manhandled. I had two ladies attack me with a tape measure. I could hear the tsk-tsking in their heads.

Clerk: You're not getting any support from that bra.
Me: Yeah, that's what I'm feeling. I think my boobs are some-where around my xiphoid process.
Clerk: Is your right boob bigger than your left boob?
Me: Umm ...
Clerk: Mine is! This one is bigger than this one ...

Right about this moment Alex peeled off and pretended he didn't know us. He started looking for a chair, couldn't find one, and I found him later, standing helplessly by the rack of menopausal, sweat-wicking nightgowns.

They loaded me up with choices in the dressing room, and Alex hunkered down in a corner on the floor near the dressing room. His night got worse, because the saleswoman went into the dressing room with me and helped me decide which bra made my boobs look best. I'd try one on, she'd tell me to show my husband, and I'd crack the door to let him take a look at the goods. His idea of a dream shopping trip was turning into his worst nightmare, and he kept muttering, "Looks good," without lifting his eyes to look at me.

We ran out of time, had to make a choice fast to get to group, and I tossed the winner to him and told him to please pay for that while I got back together. We were twenty minutes late to group, but the girls were secure, and when I was being body slammed at the conference all weekend, I was glad for my newfound support.

Something Deeper

Full-frontal hugging is a physical manifestation of something deeper and spiritual. It's about vulnerability, the willingness to open yourself to another person. In *The Gifts of Imperfection*, Brene Brown writes, "Staying vulnerable is a risk we have to take if we want to experience connection."[2]

> Full-frontal hugging is a physical manifestation of something deeper and spiritual.

The desired level of vulnerability varies from mom to mom. It depends on your level of comfort with opening up. Generally, the more vulnerable you are, the deeper your relationship will go. If you're looking for someone with whom to hang out and talk about kids, then you can stay in a safe zone and achieve that. If you're looking for that person you can call when your world's falling apart and you need someone to tell you the absolute truth, then that's going to take deeper sharing. The deeper you go, the more vulnerable you are, and the more you're opening yourself up to hurt. Go as slow as you need to go.

For some of us, it's easy to open up and we do it frequently. For others, it's difficult. Maybe we've been hurt deeply in the past and the scar is still there. Maybe our life isn't neat and tidy and we're afraid of judgment. Maybe we come from reserved stock and our people do not open up to just anybody. Whatever the reasons, sometimes people need time to build trust and to feel safe.

I am a self-professed hug-slut and tell my life to everyone on the internet. These are my people. You might feel more comfortable with a less invasive approach. When it comes to hugging and sharing, be yourself and respect the other mom if she needs to go slower than you're used to. I also have close friends who are non-huggers. They are as deep as anybody else, just more physically reserved. When they give me a hug, I receive it as a rare and valuable gift.

All Our Messy Glory

Sometimes the circumstances surrounding a date lead to a deeper level of vulnerability. Sometimes we don't have enough poise or enough time to put into place the façades behind which we hide.

The first time I went to third base with Donna, I left my house exactly how it usually is. Exactly. Usually when I know friends are coming over, especially people who haven't seen my house before, I at least scrape the dishes out of the way and throw the kids' dirty clothes in their hampers. This time, I just had her over cold turkey, no cleanup. Our second-base story time at the library date transitioned to third base because I didn't want it to end. I asked her back to my place, and as she walked into the heart of my house, she saw breakfast dishes encrusted with syrup and eggs all over one half of the countertop. The other half was covered with enough mail and paperwork to qualify us for the show *Hoarders*, and the table was covered in dirty dishes. (How many dishes do we use? At the time, we only had one child. I do not know how this was possible.) And my son's jammies were piled on the floor right where I'd peeled them off of him that morning.

Donna has a very deadpan way of saying things, and she looked around and said, "I like your house." It is what it is, friend. This is my reality.

That kicked off an entire year of weekly playdates, as our sons were the only two three-year-olds in the tri-county area who didn't attend preschool. (I adore preschool — not knocking preschool.) While our boys completely trashed my house, we did everything from a twelve-week Bible study on the book of Esther to geeking out together on jigsaw puzzles. I treasure that time together, and I never did clean my house. A few months ago when we put that house up for sale, another friend grabbed our snazzy flyer with the glossy photos on it and asked Donna if our house really looked like that inside. She hesitated and said, "Yeeeaahh. It's usually not that clean."

> **Via Twitter @UnexpectedMel**
>
> Diggin out of a crapload of disorganization & want to go back to bed. I'm channeling Jennifer Garner in 13GoingOn30: "I need a fluffy pillow!"

We need those friends who can see our homes in all their messy glory, who can see us wearing jammie pants and no makeup. If you can trust them with your real face, that's a step to trusting them with your real life. We need friends who can see our homes and faces when they're messy, and we need friends who can see our parenting and marriages when they're messy.

We aren't just dating moms to help pass the time while our kids are little. That's part of it, that's a perk, but there's more. We date moms and do life together, so that when life gets hard, we have support. We have people who truly know us and are invested in us and love us no matter what. We have people who will kick off their shoes, crawl down into the trench with us, and hold us together.

> We aren't just dating moms to help pass the time while our kids are little ... We ... do life together, so that when life gets hard, we have support.

Freezer Babies

I kept two of my babies in a freezer for two years. That makes me sound like a serial killer, but in the world of infertility treatments and in vitro fertilization, freezing babies is an actual thing. After God made Elliott in a test tube in a lab, the scientists stuck him up my vahooey with a giant turkey baster and we saw him swish into my uterus on the ultrasound monitor. It was very romantic, if you think strangers pushing on your bladder while you have to pee is up there with Barry White or "Nights in White Satin."

While Elliott was finding his way inside my fluffy endometrial lining, a nurse handed me a clipboard to sign that surprised me with two additional embryos. We didn't think we had any more, so I excitedly signed off on their frozen existence and whispered to them, "I'll be back."

When Elliott was two months old, we made our way from Washington, D.C., to Atlanta, GA, but I never forgot about my freezer babes. I weaned Elliott at thirteen months and waited the obligatory two months after breastfeeding to start the butt shots and hormonal juggernaut of in vitro all over again. Commuting from the south side of Atlanta to the north side for monitoring, I then made two trips to Washington, where they thawed out my babies and I was re-turkey bastered.

For two years, I'd prayed for and dreamed about my little babes, Elliott's frozen siblings. When the scientists thawed them out, they were alive and raring to get on in my uterus. They'd survived the frozen tundra, so now all they had to do was burrow into my carefully prepared womb.

Over the next couple of weeks, I experienced changes to my body similar to what I'd experienced with Elliott. My hope grew into confidence, and I shared with our families that I was sure I was pregnant again.

I wasn't. All the feelings I'd felt were the meds, all just the shots. I called to tell Rose the bad news. She'd just found out that she was pregnant, and I had to tell her we wouldn't get to walk that road together.

She immediately offered meals, offered to coordinate meals, offered any way she could help. I was fine. I was so fine. I wasn't sick. I could totally cook.

Over the next hour or two, the reality of no babies, no pregnancy hit me and I called her back. I wasn't fine. I was devastated. While the miscarriage was at the very beginning of the pregnancy, those babies had been in a freezer and in my heart for two years. And there weren't any more coming. My body was done.

We date moms so that we have support when life gets hard. In those first days and in those months after losing my babies, God held me together through Rose. She let me talk, she let me cry, she let me maniacally give her all my maternity clothes in some kind of macabre trunk show of all the reasons why I loved each piece and how I wanted her to have them. She even wore my pants, even though I'm like a foot and a half shorter than she is and she looked like a Marsh-wiggle from Narnia.

She found me a counselor when I couldn't quit being sad and she gently nudged me to find a healthy place. And never, ever once, not once in my presence did she ever complain about her pregnancy. She could've. Pregnancy isn't easy. Her body hurt. But she always talked about it as a gift and treated my pain with gentleness and respect.

Even though she was on a mountaintop with her long-awaited third child, she joined me in the ashes in my trench and stood by my side while I crawled out.

Sometimes momlationships are for whiling away the long hours at ballet class, and sometimes they're for helping us learn how to laugh again.

Notes

1. "Teacher's Pet," *Buffy the Vampire Slayer*, WB Television Network, aired March 24, 1997.

2. Brene Brown, *The Gifts of Imperfection: Let Go of Who You Think You're Supposed to Be and Embrace Who You Are* (Center City, Minnesota: Hazelden, 2010), 53.

Part 4

FOURTH BASE

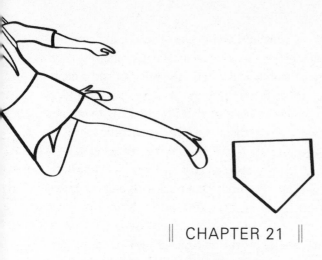

CHAPTER 21

Fourth-Basers, the Ultimate Friends

Virginia Venit: "I thought we were going to be just friends."
Happy Gilmore: "What? Friends listen to 'Endless Love' in
the dark."   From *Happy Gilmore*[1]

My husband says I should call this base "home base," and to that I say, what was I thinking writing a book based on a sports metaphor?!?! Fourth base, home run, home plate, that big diamond thingy in front of the squatting guy wearing the beetle costume, whatever. Let's talk about our homers.

That breathless feeling of driving in the dark to meet a friend. We moms of small children don't get out of the house past seven very often. You spend all day in Toddler Town, wrangle the little dears into bed in the vicinity of sevenish (or sometimes elevenish if you've had one of those days) then collapse in an exhausted heap, feeling like you can't move and you want a glass of wine but it's so far and the couch is so comfy and maybe if you send telepathic thoughts to your husband in the other room he might go pour it for you and bring it to you and maybe massage your feet and there could be chocolate and maybe a gentle fan and a cozy blanket and there you go fantasizing again. (I've heard rumors that Teen Town is equally exhausting, but I'm choosing to ignore them and stay delightfully naïve. If you're the mother of a teenager, never, ever tell me the truth. I receive your lies with blissful ignorance and blind hope for the future. Keep 'em coming, friends.)

Via Twitter @UnexpectedMel

The sound of my husband putting the kids to bed . . . so HOT.

So when you put a date on the calendar to meet a mom at a restaurant and work it out with your husband or babysitter to handle the bedtime routine, sometimes the biggest obstacle to the evening is just finding the energy to put on clean clothes, grab your purse, and walk out the front door. Usually when I'm getting ready to go out on a mom date, I waffle between the glorious anticipation of laughing with my friend without interruptions from our kids and kicking myself for scheduling it because I'm too tired to move.

As soon as I start to pull out of the driveway in our little car, the one without the car seats, and drive down our street in total silence, a wave of giddiness washes over me and I can't believe I'm actually doing this. I feel a little too cool for school, and I love my life so hard I start to choke. I adore my friends.

Via Twitter @UnexpectedMel

Spilled coffee on my jammie pants when I took a speed bump in the van too fast at the kids' school. Might have to change into actual pants.

We find each other in the lobby of the Thai place we love, the one with dim lighting and cozy booths, where they never rush us and always know our orders, even if it's been a while. Of course we start by telling each other how great we look, because that's what girls do, and after all, we dressed up for each other. Yes, these are my jeans with the sparkly pockets on the butt that I pulled out of the back of my closet. This is a dry-clean only blouse, because no one here is going to blow her nose on it. My fancy clothes.

> Yes, these are my jeans with the
> sparkly pockets on the butt that I pulled
> out of the back of my closet.

So enjoy the obligatory *we look hot* moment. Cuz you do. You so do. You are hot mamas on the loose. Full-frontal hug it out.

And then the talking. Oh, the talking. It's been weeks, or maybe months, and you only have the one night, and everyone has to have her turn, so you just launch at each other. You might need to warm up with some tongue twisters on the drive over. Maybe borrow your child's copy of *Fox in Socks* to really loosen up your tongue. We mamas can talk *fast*.

One of the funniest things about moms is that we're used to talking over the dull roar of our kids all day long. Put us in a quiet restaurant with cloth napkins and we can't help but speak at the volume level to which we're accustomed. I catch us shouting at each other across the booth. And if you're like me, when you get with your girlfriends, you aren't exactly using words that the whole restaurant needs to hear.

Maybe white tablecloths and a bowl of fancy soup isn't your jam. Maybe it's jammies. I can get equally excited about driving to a friend's house after the kiddos are in bed and watching a movie, working a puzzle, or just talking while we drink coffee and eat brownies in our jammies. You heard me. Work a puzzle. What, am I the only nerd here?

Mom dates at home are great, especially if you need a babysitter to get out, because you can take turns on hosting and hiring sitters, and cash flow doesn't keep you from getting together. And jammies. Jammies are always good, because actual clothes can be overwhelming after seven o'clock at night when you were up with a colicky baby or stressed-out teenager the night before.

Whether we're getting fancy at a cloth napkin restaurant, getting sweaty on a walk around the lake, or eating brownies together at home, fourth-base dates can restore our energy, give us laughter, and provide a break in the routine.

Know and Be Known

When you've made it to fourth base, you've arrived. You know each other and you still like each other. One of the basic needs that we have is to be known, and not just known, but understood. In *The Gifts of Imperfection*, Brene Brown writes,

> *We cultivate love when we allow our most vulnerable and powerful selves to be deeply seen and known, and when we honor the spiritual connection that grows from that offering with trust, respect, kindness and affection.*[2]

We want people to know us and we want to know other people. I want fourth-base friends who extend me grace when I don't quite say something the right way, who know what I mean, who understand my idiosyncrasies and weirdness and still want to be my friend because they see something in me worth knowing. And I want to do the same for them.

Grace for Losers

I have an overzealous gag reflex that's actually getting worse with age. When my kids throw up, it's all I can do not to join them, like I'm a contestant in the pie-eating contest from *Stand By Me*. I wasn't always this wimpy. My teeny preemie son couldn't keep anything down for about the first eighteen months of his life. Geysers of milk would erupt out of him, and somehow I survived. But now that I'm removed from the daily dairysplosions, I've become a sympathy barfer.

When I met a friend for lunch and her two-year-old launched nuggets across the tile floor, I crawled underneath the table to get away, throwing over my shoulder, "I'll go get a mop, some help, away." This same friend has an adorable little wide-eyed baby, the most precious bundle of giggling bliss. And he spits up. A lot. I want to tell him, "Hon, your mama worked hard to make that liquid gold. Now keep it down!" Every time it comes back up, I have to turn my head and think about tea tree oil and eucalyptus and ocean breezes.

I'm a total loser. And I'm grateful for my friend who loves me even though I dry heave every time her baby spits up. If we were on first, I would not be making it to second, so praise God for fourth-basers with all their grace and understanding.

On fourth, you know each other's strengths and weaknesses, and you encourage and shore up accordingly. Fourth is for opinions shared in safety, disagreements worked through lovingly, and times when you just don't have to explain.

Via Twitter @UnexpectedMel

Fourth-basers never let each other wear mom jeans. They just don't.

There's a code. No gossiping. Total trustworthiness. Grace for her quirks and failings. If she needs you, you're there, whether it's a texted prayer or a midnight vigil. Fourth-basers snort laugh together, cultivate inside jokes in the fertile soil of shared humor, and aren't afraid to let each other know when there's a wayward booger whistling in and out of a nostril or a stray piece of kale stuck between teeth.

When your life falls off the edge and into a trench, fourth-basers don't just throw you a rope. They crawl down in the trench with you. If your marriage is on metaphorical life support, if your parent is on actual life support, if your kids are cracking at the center, if you're fighting depression, demons, or disaster, fourth-base friends wade into the muck and hold you up.

They are not our Jesus. But he can use them to speak truth into our lives and hold us together when we're falling apart. My friends aren't my Savior, but sometimes he uses them to point me to him when I can't find my way.

Play 'n' Pray

I get together with two friends almost every week, Amy and Rory. Between the three of us, our kids come from five continents. While I'm still in the wee years, they have kids ranging from newborn to college. Sometimes I can't believe they want to hang out with me.

Our kids play together while we solve the world's problems and pray. A playdate with prayer, a play 'n' pray, if you will. Sometimes our prayers last for an hour. Sometimes ten minutes. Sometimes our daughters crawl into our laps while we pray. Evie cups my face in her hands and I hear her saying quiet words to God while Rory offers up words across our little circle.

When I felt a stirring to write more, write louder, I confided in them with shaky uncertainty. I felt

> **Via Twitter @UnexpectedMel**
>
> Evie: Can you pray for my ear?
>
> Me: Sure! God, please heal Evie's ear. Thank you for creating our bodies to heal —
>
> Evie: That's enough prayer.

compelled, like I had to do this brave thing, but I was terrified and silenced by my own insignificance. They prayed over my words, over my heart. They "liked" every post and status, from the beginning, when they were the only ones. And they challenged me and reminded me of why I write when I felt like giving up and wondered who would care about a somewhat reformed f-bomb-dropping orphan care advocate who laughs at poop jokes.

Amy encouraged me to ask the Lord for a verse, something to which I could cling when I felt fearful and not enough and small. I did ask, and the next day, he answered.

> My salvation and my honor depend on God;
> he is my mighty rock, my refuge.
>
> PSALM 62:7

We need momlationships because they help us to be brave. They give us strength to stick up for our kids when they're drowning in school, to chase the dreams that glitter like diamonds nestled in our souls, to fight for truth and justice for the kid down the street or the kid across the world. They remind us that we're not alone, and we're doing a good life's work. My friends provide a safe place to wrestle with faith questions and marriage questions and parenting questions.

Friends are fallible. They have their own lives. They are not our Jesus and we cannot suck all the life out of them in an effort to feel whole and loved. So we won't put all our faith and hope in them, but we will appreciate the incredible support and encouragement they provide.

When I think about going out with other moms, two things come to mind, being dressed and laughing. The image is just there instantly. And it makes me happy. Mom dates create an occasion to get dressed up in something cute and always result in belly-hurting laughter.

But as I ponder, fact of the matter is, there are not many mom dates for me anymore. Not for lack of moms in my life. But they stress me out. The dates, not the moms. And I am usually exhausted by the end of them.

You see, mom dates stress me out because all too often the conversation turns toward my daughter and the challenges we wade through daily with her. She has battled seizures since we adopted her and since then, it has been a main theme in our lives. And when I start talking about it, and hear myself sharing my heart cry, I feel like that needy friend. The mom of the special child who everyone wants to pat her hand and give her a look I can't even put a name to and I hate that. It makes me feel like I am on the outside of "normal" moms. And feeling on the outside is something I have struggled with for years. Like the third wheel on a very awkward bicycle.

So while moms are talking about their jobs, about their kid's accomplishments, their common colds, pregnancies, maternity fashions, upcoming playdates, and other "normal" things, I feel like an outsider. So I listen and try to agree and always keep a smile on my face. It takes energy sometimes. It takes energy always.

And then someone will see I have been absent from conversation for a while and turn and ask, "What about you? What's going on with you?" or "How are things with Abby?" Sometimes there is not even a "What about you?" because so much of our life is about Abby.

And so I quickly ponder the response. And that takes energy. Do I give the, "Oh . . . we are fine. Taking it a day at a time," with the smile and nod and turn the conversation elsewhere? Or do I give a tiny crumb of truth and say, "We are still struggling with seizures, but we are good"?

Or do I lay it out there and say, "She had six seizures last night. I am not sleeping. I am struggling with anger and bitterness because she is so disrespectful while I pour myself out to her and I feel like a terrible person for the majority of time"?

Well. Hello, Debbie Downer. WHO invited you to the party? And it is just downhill from there.

See, I don't want to be that person. I am the outgoing, happy, positive, encouraging, giving one in the group. Not the needy one.

And so I come home exhausted. Exhausted from being THAT girl when everything in me screams, "I AM NOT THAT GIRL!"

And that leads me to this.

There is an inner circle of friends with whom I can be real and NOT feel like Debbie Downer . . . because they understand. There is SOME common thread that connects us and I am safe there. I have about three in that inner circle that hold my arms up when I can no longer lift a finger.

They know when to come in closer. They know when I need space. They know when to hand me a tissue. They know when to smack me back into truth.

They get me. They don't pity me. They know the me who is not THAT mom. And they love me.

And when I come home from one of those mom dates, I feel like I am not on the outside, but I am in! I am accepted. And I know I can keep going forward.

I am learning to embrace being BOTH those moms, the giving one and the needy one. And I am so very thankful to have an inner circle of moms to help me swim in the grace of it all. — *Dawn S.*

Notes

1. *Happy Gilmore*, directed by Dennis Dugan, Universal Pictures, 1996.
2. Brene Brown, *The Gifts of Imperfection: Let Go of Who You Think You're Supposed to Be and Embrace Who You Are* (Center City, Minnesota: Hazelden, 2010), 26.

|| CHAPTER 22 ||

Cranking Out a Mom Date If It Kills You

Charles De Mar: "Go that way, really fast. If something gets in your way, turn."   From *Better Off Dead*[1]

So you've arrived, you're in love, and you want her in your life. At this point, it's about maintenance. How do you maintain your momlationship? How do you balance the needs of your kids, your spouse, your job, your family, your volunteer work, your everything else, with this friendship? Because let's be honest, for many of us, when things get tough, our friendships are one of the first things to suffer. How can we walk through life together and not lose our besties when things get hard?

You know those friends whose schedules are somehow polar opposite of yours and you just can't seem to find time to get together and you keep planning things and it just won't work? Sometimes you have to pull back, and sometimes you have to just crank it out because you love that mama too much.

The Drop-Off Meal Date

One of the primary enemies of the mom date is the Sick Child. You don't see it coming. You're powerless against it. Sick Child springs out of nowhere and your plans are shot. If a friend has to cancel on you because of Sick Child, grab that opportunity to fetch her a latte and drive it over. If it's anything involving vomit, maybe just leave it on the doorstep and don't share air space. Bringing a friend a little pick-me-up when she's bumming hard about her big night out being exploded to pieces goes a long way to letting her know how much you care. "In sickness and in health" ... oh wait, that's a different relationship.

> One of the primary enemies of the
> mom date is the Sick Child.

You can also bring dinner. When I moved to the Deep South, I discovered this beautiful world of meal making. I mean, in the North, I'd experienced making meals for people, but these girls bump it up to a whole new level. When someone has a baby down here, sometimes they have meals delivered for two months. Southern hospitality is a real thing.

No matter where you live, if your friend has a sick child, she might spend the whole day at the doctor's office, pharmacy, and cleaning up after the little sicko. When she cancels on you, tell her you're bringing dinner. Sometimes when I don't have time to cook, I just swing by the store and pick up breakfast or snack items, a rotisserie chicken, or something with B-A-K-E-R-Y on it so my friend doesn't have to think about feeding the rest of her kids.

Part of being a good friend is serving. When we serve each other, it deepens our love and commitment to each other. When I'm at the store, I like to pick up cards for friends too. In our world of texting and Facebook, it's special when we receive a card in the actual mailbox. Of course, you have to grab her address without appearing creepy, but by fourth base, you probably know her address or won't appear too stalkerish asking for it.

> When you are in the military, having mom friends saves your sanity. There are unique challenges that come with being a military spouse. Having friends who know what you are going through without you having to explain it is really helpful. There are deployments, trips that last for weeks, training where you and your spouse are separated for months, times when missions are classified and you don't know where they are, or when they are coming home. It is so helpful to have friends who have been through the same things. They know the questions to ask, the ones not to ask, and when you just need someone to come hold your crying baby so you can take a twenty-minute nap, because you haven't slept in days. They just get it, no explanation needed. I am so thankful for the mom friends that I have from the military. They are strong, amazing women. — *Melissa N.*

The Breakfast Date

Our lives are completely, ridiculously insane, are they not? I honestly don't know how we fit as much into one day as we do. Some weeks we don't have a single evening free, and how's a girl supposed to get in a mom date with soccer-baseball-lacrosse-basketball practice and Awana-Girl-Boy Scout Club and ballet-swimming lessons and tutoring-mathletes-homework? It's impossible. Let's just give up.

Or. If you're having a hard time scheduling a fourth-base date at night, have you met my little friend the Breakfast Date? This requires a bit of prep work the night before, buttering up your husband or responsible teenager to handle the morning routine and laying out outfits, packing lunches, getting everything ready the night before, but it could be worth it. There could be pancakes.

Arrange to meet your fourth-base friend at your favorite, open-early breakfast joint or coffee shop, and while the kids are sleeping, groggily rolling out of bed, and pulling on their clothes, you could be enjoying an hour of uninterrupted conversation with syrup. I usually feel like the sweaty part of a butt cheek when I'm pulling out of the driveway and it's still dark outside and I wonder why I would ever choose to get up earlier than I have to, but once I'm sitting with my mom date stuffing my face with coffee, I love my life again. That hour gives me energy for the rest of the day and reminds me why I bother to leave the house at all. The point of all this is that the mamas in my life make me a better person. They get my head on straight. Hopefully I'm performing the same service for them.

For the breakfast date, I give you permission to wear your jammies. If you're meeting a fourth-base date, then she can handle this. And if I hear about a lot of makeup going on, I'm gonna hunt you down. The Breakfast Date doesn't need makeup and actual clothes. The Breakfast Date enjoys the pile of clothes next to your side of the bed from the night before. The Breakfast Date doesn't even need your teeth brushed, as long as you both agree not to use a lot of words that start with *H*.

The Big Tureen of Coffee Date

Rose and I talk about coffee like frat boys talk about beer.

Rose: Dude, yo, we're gonna drink so much coffeeee.

Me: I know, right? I'm gonna drink so much my hands shake.

Rose: That'll be sweet. I'm gonna just keep refilling my cup while we're talking, and we're just gonna talk and drink coffee, like, all morning long.

Me: Dude. That's so awesome.

Rose: Shah.

Dear all the frat boys, I'm sorry. I may have mixed you up with Bill and Ted of *Excellent Adventure* fame.

The main rule of the coffee date is that if you and she are both holding coffee mugs, then wherever you are, it can, by the official guidelines of this book of mom dating, be considered a legit mom date. No matter where you are, what you're wearing, or from where the coffee originated.

Side-by-side sifting through the racks at the consignment sale while your kids are in Mom's Morning Out, with coffee, equals date. Shop fast, talk faster. Fourth-base friends should know how each other drinks her coffee too. Make sure you cover that ahead of time. Black, cream and sugar, or froofy foamy thing. Important.

Via Twitter @UnexpectedMel

Just drank a cup of tea. Don't tell coffee I cheated on him. It was one time. It didn't mean anything. It just happened.

If you're really desperate for some fourth-base connecting, offer to bring her a cup and meet in the school parking lot before pickup. Twenty minutes, hug it out, talk it up, drink it down.

Tea drinkers, you can play too. My fabulous Martha is a tea drinker, and I adore her. There is forgiveness and grace in the kingdom of God, even for drinking tea.

The Smelly Minivan Date

I can't say enough how much I adore my rolling petri dish, the room in my house that never gets cleaned, my dear yucky van. I love my van! And I will totally invite you to drive somewhere in it if we're on fourth.

Via Facebook @UnexpectedMel

While cleaning out the van, a sippy cup from two months ago spilled dubious yellow liquid all over the backseat. Also noteworthy — desiccated apple core, additional cup sporting black mold, something squishy that made me gag. Time to pick up my mom date.

Dating isn't just about the destination, it's about the journey, and when you live in the suburbs like I do, the journey can take a while. The last thing I want to do is waste solid mom-date time driving by myself. Get in, buckle up, and talk to me.

Do you need to drive to the big, bad city for something?

Via Twitter @UnexpectedMel

On my mom date, she grabbed a pen in the van door & squealed, "Ew! It's greasy!" Don't ever stick your hand in a crack in my van.

Me too. Get in. Are you running errands this morning? Me too. Get in my van. I'll brush the crushed cereal off the seat. Your coffee is welcome, and feel free to spill it.

The Movie Date

There's finding a fourth-base friend, and then there's finding a fourth-base friend with the same taste in movies. Dude. I mean, really? Especially if your movie taste tends to skew toward the sci-fi, superhero, action side of things like mine does. Those women are one in a thousand, at least. I was raised by a sci-fi mama and I've become a sci-fi mama, but we are a rare breed.

One of my favorite dates is a movie date with Donna. There isn't a sci-fi reference I throw down that she doesn't get immediately. It's geek mom love at its warp core.

Our local theater does discounted movie tickets on Tuesday nights, with free refills on popcorn and slushies, and yeah, heck yeah, we've been known to grab a doubleheader. Get there early, polish off a popcorn and slushie before the movie starts, refill, watch first movie, refill again, watch second movie, use time in between movies to catch up and talk nerd to each other.

It's fabulous and just writing about it makes me want to ask her out right now. It's the kind of thing we'll anticipate for a whole week, and she's already asked me out for a movie coming out in two months.

If you aren't a geek, the movie date is still available to you. Anything Tina Fey or in the Fey-verse will do, or explore your deep love for all things Latifah.

And if you can't leave the house, you can still accomplish this date with the kids in bed and a whole lot of Netflix. In fact, Donna and I had a *Doctor Who* marathon a few weeks ago. When she arrived at my house, we discovered that Netflix was broken.

Broken. Not just our system. The whole Netflix. How does that even happen?!? It's like breaking the internet. And why that night, when it had been forever and we'd worked out our schedules with the hubbies, and we needed a *Who*-fix stat.

I was ready to turn into a Weeping Angel if I didn't get to see them on a screen when we realized that we could still stream Netflix through my computer. We are so pathetic that we huddled around my desk in uncomfortable chairs all evening watching old episodes of the Tenth Doctor and eating coconut oil kettle corn. Cranking it out.

The Grocery Store Date

Everyone has to go grocery shopping. Instead of schlepping your kids around by yourself, invite another mom to join you. One of my favorite mom dates is throwing the kids in the minivan and driving up to Trader Joe's in Atlanta. For us suburbanites, this is a bit of a haul. And I can't take credit for this date idea.

Rose introduced me to the world of the grocery store date. Throw the kids in the van, grab coffee for you and donuts for them, and talk like mad all the way to the store. Gesture with your hands, solve the world's problems, and don't let the kids suck you into their backseat drama.

> **Via Twitter @UnexpectedMel**
> Grocery mom date. During the car ride we covered govt shutdown, marriage, dealing w/whiny girls & our love of salty things. #momstalkfast

When you get there, swing by the park down the street, let them run out all their energy, then when everyone has to go to the bathroom, hop back in the van, head to the grocery, drain bladders, and push your carts around the store together.

At a place like Trader Joe's, you also have the benefit of the little sample bar in the corner. I buy snacks and drink boxes, get everyone back in the van, and head home, and if you grab frozen pizzas or tacos or something equally easy, you can keep the togetherness going with an easy lunch date back at the house.

What's the other place we like to frequent? Target. Next time you're headed to Target, see if a friend needs anything and arrange to meet at the entrance. Bonus if your Target has a Starbucks in the front. (I know I sound soooo suburban right now. If you're a city mom, forgive me. I picture you at the Whole Foods, then strolling to a local coffee shop ... someone should start a City-Suburb-Rural Mom "day-in-the-life" swap so we can check out each others' lives.)

I love finding ways to just "do life" together. We all have these things that we do, over and over. A simple run to get more toilet paper can turn into a chance to catch up and combine crazies. My kids love getting sneak attack time with their friends too, and they all destroy a display of paper towels while I hear about a friend's new part-time job.

Dear all the places I shop,

I'm sorry about the destroyed displays. And also, all the candy and crappery in the check-out lanes is just asking for it, and you get what you deserve with those things.

Love, Melanie

Notes

1. *Better Off Dead*, directed by Savage Steve Holland, A&M Films, 1985.

|| CHAPTER 23 ||

Praying for a Bromance

Turk: "You ask me 'bout this thing we share ..."

J.D.: "... and he tenderly replies."

Turk: "It's guy love ..."

J.D. & Turk: "... between two guys."

From Scrubs[1]

For married moms, what's the one thing that's even better than a fourth-base friend? A fourth-base couple.

Clara and I discovered that our kids were in the same pre-school class and we went to the same church. We started helping each other out in the pickup line after school, and our kids were both new to the preschool, so we had each other as wing-women at class parties when all the other moms already knew each other.

I started wading into the whole gluten-/dairy-free thing with Elliott, and Clara had walked that road already, so she became a tremendous resource for me as I perused new aisles at the grocery store and discovered that if I wasn't careful, my grocery bill was going to triple. We became food allergy buddies and bonded over our shared experience of doing high school in the early to mid-nineties.

One night, we realized we both had babysitters for date night with our husbands and decided to see the same movie. This was it. Our husbands had met, but now we were combining forces for an evening of merriment. Would we all survive it? Our dates became a double, and after the movie, the four of us stood outside in the parking lot for so long talking that we decided to follow it up with coffee. We all just clicked.

Since then, our families have done movie nights, dinners, and after-church lunches where our kids destroy a restaurant while we try to talk. We've actually started moving our post-church swath of destruction to an in-house Crock-Pot situation to relieve both our wallets and the local restaurants with children's menus.

We've done a weekend in the mountains, and we regularly take our canoes out together. I can't imagine life without us all together, and it's all because our hubbies have the kind of bromance they write songs about, if they wrote songs about bromance. Late at night, Clara and I find our guys playing Call of Duty together with their headsets on, and they take full-frontal hugging to a whole new level involving trying to squeeze the air out of each other and a lot of guy-love backslapping.

> Our hubbies have the kind of bromance
> they write songs about ...

They're adorable. My husband works from home and never leaves the house, but when he hears that Clara's hubby wants to do something, he's like a little boy riding his bike to the neighbor's house.

Clara and I still do our fourth-base dates, but more often than not, we end up taking the guys along because they're just too excited about each other to stay home. And then recently, our husbands cut *us* out of the equation and hooked up for a kayak adventure. Very bromantic.

When your fourth-baser is amazing and things are going well, when do you try to hook up your husbands? Don't force it. Let it evolve. Let your momlationship grow and thrive before you add in the hubby x-factor. That way if they have zero to talk about and act like the worst versions of themselves, at least you have each other.

The movie night was a good test, because the majority of the night we watched a great film. No talking. Clara and I sat in the middle, with hubbies flanking us on either side. Minimal participation required, just getting used to the idea of the four of us. After the movie, we had a built-in subject about which to talk, the movie that we just saw.

And standing in the parking lot, as we talked and laughed and talked and laughed and realized that hey, these people are really fun and we kinda don't want to stop talking and laughing, then a nearby coffee shop was a great way to continue the conversation.

One thing I've learned from my husband is that most guys don't want to sit around just talking. They need an activity. I'm not speaking for everyone of course, but if your man is anything like my husband and his friends, you might want to keep that in mind. When the guys are involved, we're usually on the lake, lighting off fireworks, lighting something on fire, or at least watching a funny movie. And eating. Always with the food eating.

> Most guys don't want to sit around just talking.
> They need an activity.

So if you're thinking about dealing in the husbands to your momlationship, think activities. Poker might be a good one, but only if you're a better poker player than I am. Early in our marriage, my husband tried to let me play poker with him and I am not cool enough to bluff people with my face. I'm all, "Oooh, wheee, lookie what I got!" And also, "Wait, I forget. What's a flush? Do I have one?" My husband was ready to flush *me*.

When your husbands have a passionate bromance, you end up with a lot of family dating, like our annual jammie night with Rose's family, where we celebrate Jesus' birth with fondue.

Nothing says *Feliz Navidad* like rye bread dunked in melted beer cheese. I'm not sure what to say about two grown men wearing onesies together. If there's an age limit on footie jammies, they are not aware of it.

> I'm not sure what to say about two grown men wearing onesies together.

One thing Rose and I have learned over the years is that our husbands are smarter than we are. After dinner, they disappear into the man cave while we wrangle all the kids we've seen all the dang long day. If you want any time to have a conversation on a family date, you have to disappear faster than your husbands. After the final bite hits your lips, leave the dishes and vamoose. Take the man cave by force if you have to. Try, "Here, could you hold Khan Jr. for a sec?" Then run away faster than brave Sir Robin.

Now, what do you do if your husbands are a train wreck together? It happens. Sometimes, the magic you have with your girlfriend just doesn't happen between your husbands. The two of you connect with the shared joys and challenges of motherhood, your love of books or sushi or yoga, and your total devotion to the complete works of *The Gilmore Girls*. Husbands don't have *The Gilmore Girls*, and that makes it harder for them. Maybe one hubby roots for the Dolphins and the other hubby swims with the dolphins and they have nothing to talk about.

Fear not. Your momlationship will survive, and now you have an excellent child care option built in for your fourth-base dates. Your husbands will be so thrilled not to have to spend time together that they'll willingly stay home and put the kiddos to bed while you go out.

Notes

1. "My Musical," *Scrubs*, National Broadcasting Company, aired January 18, 2007.

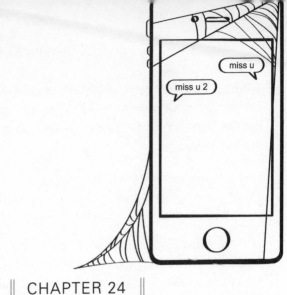

CHAPTER 24

Rekindling the Momlationship

Charlie Mackenzie: " 'He wants you back,' he screamed into the night air like a fireman going to a window that has no fire … except the passion of his heart. I am lonely. It's really hard. This poem … sucks." From *So I Married an Axe Murderer*[1]

It's been a while. You've blown her off a few times. She's blown you off. Life is kicking your butt and you can barely remember the names of your kids. You vaguely recollect when you were kind of fun but have no idea how to get back to that and wonder if she'd even pick up the phone if you tried.

If I've given off any false vibe that I have my own momlationships completely together, let me swish away that desert mirage. The most terrifying thing about writing a book about relationships with women is the fear that everyone in my life will come forward and rat me out as the bad friend that I am. I love my momlationships, but I don't always get them right. Sometimes if our kids are no longer in shared activities, then time goes by and I realize I have no idea how their lives are going. They could be in the hospital. They could be in jail. And they have no idea about my own impending jail time or hospitalization. So here are some things I've done to rekindle the relationships I've let drop in the craziness of life.

Write her a note. Drop a card in the mail. Tell her how you feel, that you miss her like crazy, and be specific. What do you miss? What do you love about her? Why are you grateful to have her in your life?

Follow up with a phone call. Text her when something you see makes you think of her. Offer up a couple different times in the next week when you can get together and see if she'll pick one or offer another one back.

Don't give up. Sometimes you just have to stoke those friendship fires before they go out. If you have ten minutes in the car waiting for your kids or driving to pick them up, use that time to call her, catch up, and phone-hug it out. Sometimes when life is crazy and I haven't spoken to a friend for a while, I just leave a message on her voice mail, letting her know that I love her and miss her.

One of my good friends was overdue with her baby at the same time that I was buying plane tickets to go get our daughter. In a burst of extremely gross multitasking, I had the following text conversation while, um, well, going to the bathroom. Shut up, you've done it too. When you have small children, it's the only time you're alone.

Me: Induction?! Do I need to come up there with a pair of tongs and a spatula?

Her: Yes, induction tomorrow night — bluh!!! She must like it in here. I think she likes the food!

Me: You are hospitable ☺. Excited for the big birthday! We got our travel dates — leaving on Sunday!

Her: No way!!!!! That is sooooo great!! So happy we are getting our daughters at the same time — can't wait for them to meet! ☺

Me: Yes! You go push a watermelon out your yam. I'll go fly to
      Europe and eat Latvian chocolate. :)

Her: Yeah, I am liking your delivery a lot more than mine!!! Can
      you at least bring me some chocolate??

As I'm finishing this book and adopting my oldest daughter at the same time, I'm painfully aware that I have less and less time for the very relationships about which I'm writing. I'm working double time to try to reach out and stay connected.

So lately I've had to get creative with keeping my relationships alive. I have a couple of friends who text prayers back and forth throughout the day as we're all driving our vans all over town. Well, I mean, not *while* we're driving.

When It's on the Rocks

Texting, calling, writing cards, skywriting, whatever. And after you've tried all that ... oh crap. She isn't texting you back. She had that look on her face when you said hi at soccer practice. Or maybe she saw you at Target with another mom and looked shocked, and you wanted to scream at her a la Ross Geller, "We were on a break!"[2] How can we tell if our momlationships are on the rocks?

The question we all ask when we're completely over the moon about another mom is "Does she feel the same about me?" And when she's texting you back, and taking turns initiating getting together, and acting like she's genuinely happy to see you, you're content and at ease. But what about when things aren't flowing anymore?

First, I always try to believe the best of her. I start out staying positive and assuming there's no weirdness. Maybe she drank a bad latte. Maybe her kid threw up on her this morning and she still has the smell up her nose, which is why she's making that "I smelled something" face. Maybe she just fought with her husband. Maybe she has other friends too, and that's completely okay. Maybe lots of things before I get to "It's me."

I'm an insecure person, and I think I'm not alone in this. Many of us struggle with insecurity, especially in relationships, especially if we've been burned before. So, I have to fight to believe the best. Not fight with her. Fight with my own brain. Punch insecurity in the face, cast it out in Jesus' name, or fart on it. Whatever. Shove it away. It will only screw up your friendship.

If it's an ongoing thing and she continues to blow you off, again, believe the best and assume there's no weirdness. We all go through life stages. She's just had a baby and can barely sit down from the stitches up her hooha. She's just brought home the child she's adopted and she's trying to make a connection with a traumatized child while wading through jet lag and the little intestinal friend she picked up while abroad. She's just started a new job and is trying to keep her kids fed and picked up from school on time while undergoing a massive schedule change.

Text Support.

Being a mama is not easy.

Raising kids is hard.

Sometimes I think that the nearest equivalent to being a mama to three young boys is like conducting an orchestra on a plane that is going down.

There is too much to do.

Everything is hurried.

Everything needs attention now.

Nothing goes as planned.

I have a friend. A true mama friend. I will just refer to her as Courtney.

Her days and her family look a lot like mine. Some of her children are adopted. So are some of mine. We both love

Jesus, good food, and running. We both desire to be godly mamas. We both find it to be almost too hard sometimes.

We cope and hold each other up by texting.

Sometimes we write paragraphs.

Other times it is a single word or two. Our texts cover a variety of topics. Some are happy and encouraging, some sad and hard. Courtney has sent me all of these at some point:

> toilet
>
> principals office
>
> principals office . . . again
>
> he scored a goal!
>
> Joy-filled.
>
> Can you believe that it is just 7:12 am?

When she wrote "principals office . . . again," I knew it all, the whole entire story. My stomach was in knots too, and I only needed three little words. I stopped, immediately, and prayed for her. The very next thing I did was call Papa John's and had them bring her a pizza. Because that is what we do. Text Support.

Not that long ago, my boys flushed something down the toilet until it flooded. Naturally, before I did anything, I texted her a picture of the mess. Later that day she put a box of straws and a note in my mailbox, "When you feel like you are drowning, sometimes you just need a straw." Text Support.

In this crazy portion of life where everything is hurried and urgent and loud and nothing goes as planned, all I want is to sit on a couch and have long uninterrupted talks with friends like Courtney. But all I need is a friend who knows me well enough to make it better with a few short words of support.

Text Support. — *Megan C.*

Before you assume it's you, figure out if it's just life. If something in her life is kicking her butt, cook her a meal, mail her a card, drop off bagels on her doorstep, or offer to pick up her kids. Life stuff is the glue that brings mamas together. Our shared drama gives us an opportunity to serve our way into a deeper friendship than ever.

I try to tell myself a lot, "It's not about me." I do that because my general tendency is to assume it's all about me. If she definitely seems on the cool side and you think something's wrong, ask. Rather than having the conversation up in your own head, ask her if something is wrong. Often, that takes care of it. Boom.

Seasons and Stages

We all have different seasons and stages in life. Throughout the year, I grow closer to different moms, depending on what our kids are doing. Donna and I spent every week together when our boys were three. We playdated hard, we playdated long. We playdated each other's brains out. It was fabulous.

The following school year, we each added a new kid to our broods, plus our boys went to different preschools. She's still one of my close friends, and we are intentional about getting together for third- and fourth-base dates. However, we'll never replicate that special year when we spent all that time together. Rather than comparing what we have now to what we had then, I like to think of the quality time from then as the solid foundation for our good friendship now. Weeks can go by as we wade through our busy lives, but when we get together, it's easy and fun.

Often friendships don't end, they just change as our kids and lives change. Babies and new schools and new sports and activities always change the dynamic of a friendship. Let's be women with open hearts and open arms for the moms in front of us, always ready to welcome a new friend into our mix.

I want to be a friend who always makes room, someone who's known for openness and hospitality. I want my home and my life to invite others in. I don't always get that right, but it's my heart and what I work toward.

Truth be told, I'm independent, perhaps stubborn, a little headstrong. Maybe it's because I was dropped into this single-mom role so suddenly, that from the beginning, I've felt like I've had to do this on my own: survive the divorce, pick up the pieces, form community in a brand-new town, continue to be the mommy that my daughter needed me to be, figure out not only what single parenting looks like, but eventually co-parenting too — it's a lot of change. I've had to be so independent that I'm realizing now I'd swung too far on the pendulum. I found that my pride was disguised as independence. I had isolated myself, thinking that no one else understood where I was coming from, but it was through yet another trial that I was forced to come to the end of myself and rely on my friends for their prayers and moral support. I realized that God wasn't asking me to do this by myself. I had to place myself in a single mom's Sunday school class, remain in a Bible study, and be vulnerable with people I knew I could trust and whom I knew I would see every week. Community doesn't have to be people in your exact life situation, but it helps to have people who know where you are coming from, at least, that's where I've felt the safest. — *Rachel J.*

Notes

1. *So I Married an Axe Murderer*, directed by Tommy Schlamme, TriStar Pictures, 1993.
2. "The One with the Morning After," *Friends*, National Broadcasting Company, aired February 20, 1997.

‖ CHAPTER 25 ‖

Going Long Distance

The Doctor: "Rose, before I go, I just want to tell you: you were fantastic. Absolutely fantastic. And you know what? So was I."
From *Doctor Who*[1]

If this book had a sound track, I'd pump out "Friends" by Michael W. Smith right about now, the song that still takes me back to summer camp. "It's hard to let you go, but in the Father's hands we know, that a lifetime's not too long to live as friends."[2] Shut up, everyone cries at summer camp.

Saying good-bye. The days of camp are long gone, but saying good-bye to friends hasn't gotten any easier. When you do life with each other and your kids are best friends and you've made it to the stage when you can drop over unannounced and stay for leftover lasagna, job changes and moves can feel like abdominal surgery.

My first mom friend, my Rose-girl, moved away a few years ago, and I think she packed up part of my heart and half of my brain with her. After she told me of her upcoming move, we joked and laughed and talked about how we'd be fine. We kept our emotions light and vowed to stay positive and not focus on the ouchy part. I was a rock.

> I think she packed up part of my heart
> and half of my brain with her.

And then one night, as our families got together for dinner yet again, I carried a salad down her front walk. As I passed the For Sale sign in her yard, the tears started flowing and no matter how hard I tried, I could not suck them back in.

My husband laughs at me, because I have two modes when I'm dealing with something colossally painful. Mode One, I'm totally together and using humor as a survival tactic. I literally cannot cry in this mode. I should mention I am usually in this mode. Even if I feel emotionally constipated and dying for a good enema of the tear duct, the only things that come out are quips. I squirt out quips instead of tears and I laugh with overtones of hysteria. My father almost died a couple of years ago, like, EMTs with paddles doing the whole "Clear!" thing, and I think I was quipping by the next day. Emotionally constipated.

Mode Two, what's beyond an ugly cry? I sound like a wounded animal and emit Wookie-like sounds that land somewhere between a laugh and a cry. People around me experience confusion as they aren't sure if they should laugh with me or get me a tissue. Boogers flow freely and my keening is occasionally broken by hacking and laughing at my own ridiculousness. Whale sounds. That's what it's like. I am a humpback whale, and I make people nervous.

For months after learning about the impending move, I managed Mode One like a boss. I quipped up, down, and sideways about the state to which she was moving, and I chirped perky, supportive comments about what a great friend she is and how she'd have no trouble making new mom friends.

And then walking toward her house that fateful night, passing her For Sale sign, Mode Two hit hard. With a vengeance. I entered her house keening out my humpback Wookie noises and she tried to grab the salad bowl from me before I dripped snot into the romaine.

No matter how much we spin it, long distance sucks.

Since they moved to a galaxy far, far away, we've managed to grip our friendship and hold it together over the light-years. We've visited them a few times, they've visited us, and one time we even did a drive-by, meeting them for lunch off the interstate when we were on a road trip that came within their atmosphere. More often than not, we text quotes from old *Friends* episodes or leave quick voice mails with screaming kids in the background.

Fourth-basers can go a long time, but when you get together, it feels comfortable and like you were never apart. One thing I've found that helps my long-distance relationships is that when we are together, we make new memories, not just talk about the old ones. It's fine to reminisce about the good ol' days when we saw each other every week, but if we did only that, our relationship would stagnate over time.

> The days after she moved out of our little town were sad ones for me, but I had learned an important lesson from that friendship and I knew just what to do. I swallowed my fears, loaded up my kiddos into a wagon, and walked down the street to the house of a girl I had known for quite a while but had not yet fully friended due to my petty insecurities. I knocked on her door, and when that door opened, a new friendship was forged that would carry me on into another desperately crazy stage of life that included three more children and homeschooling. — *Carolyn M.*

So we move forward and continue to develop the relationship, albeit slowly and with distance-induced gaps. When I see photos of her on Facebook with her new rad friends, I squelch the impulse to hate them, merely for the crime of having her every day. Instead, I send her YouTube videos involving fart jokes, because they may be closer, but I will always be grosser.

Rose: I am waiting on a friend to meet us for lunch. I will forever and always think of you when I am here and miss our dates. XOXOXO

Me: Will she pound the waffle fries like me?!?!

Every few days, we text something completely random that we know the other one will just get. One time she sent me this:

Rose: Behind a car and their license plate is 2Gross ... please get that next time you have to renew!!! ☺

When Rose was pregnant with her first girl, I sent this:

Me: Biggest difference between my girl and boy: she is Always There. Talking. All day up on me talking my head off. Maybe one of your boys is like that. Elliott is not. If I had a zipper, she'd wear me like a skin suit. As I write this, she's hanging off my thighs begging to sit on my lap running her hands up and down my legs and trying to climb up me. She's almost four. Aaaagggghhhhh!!! Someday I will love this. Grateful for the connection, grateful grateful grateful! Aggghhhhh!!!!! She's trying to shove her head between my thighs now.

Rose: I'm dying laughing!!!! Oh my, having a girl is going to be SO different!! My boys do not do that—They just run off and play! Thanks for the laugh.

Then a few weeks later out of the blue:

Me: I just realized that my kids are soooooo gonna tell people that I fart all the time.

Rose: Hubby and I are on a date and we are laughing our heads off!!! Yeah, they are gonna tell! At your funeral that's how they can remember you!!!

Me: We are trapped in a car driving to Aspen for my sister-in-law's wedding and it's like my colon is launching itself out my butt. I put the ass in Aspen.

Rose: Stop and buy some fart pills. What did you eat??? Travelers' gut? Hopefully you won't poop your pants at the wedding. Better bring a backup dress.

Me: I had falafel for breakfast and black beans for lunch. On a day when I've been on a plane and in the car. My family deserves a medal. Nose hairs are GONE. I'm laughing so hard I'm crying. Alex is sure we have it in our clothes, like secondhand smoke, except farts. This poor rental car will never be the same.

Rose: We are seriously dying laughing. I have to pee so bad and I might wet my pants! We are on one last getaway overnighter before baby tonight! Thanks for the laugh!

A few days later ...

Rose: How was the wedding??
Me: Stunning.
Rose: Did your farts calm down?
Me: Yes ... I birthed a gremlin and they subsided.

I Don't Want To

I could write forever about how much I love my friends, how much I love momlationships, and why we need each other. I really, really, really don't want to write the next section. I don't want to talk about breakups, because I love women so much and breakups are sucky and painful and reveal our darker side.

I want to be all puppies and rainbows and that awkward scene in *Star Wars: Episode II—Attack of the Clones* when Padme and Anakin roll around in the meadow together. I want all the love without any of the pain.

But that's not real. We can talk all day about women linking arms and doing life together and making it work no matter what, but sometimes, sometimes it just doesn't.

Sigh. So, just for a little bit, not for too long, just long enough to acknowledge that it's a real thing, let's talk about breakups. And then get back to frolicking.

Notes

1. "The Parting of the Ways," *Doctor Who*, British Broadcasting Network, aired June 18, 2005.

2. Michael W. Smith and Deborah D., "Friends," copyright © 1982 Meadowgreen Music Company (ASCAP) (adm. at CapitolCMGPublishing.com). All rights reserved. Used by permission.

Part 5

(NOT QUITE) HOME FREE

CHAPTER 26

Breaking Up Is Hard to Do: *The Phaseout*

Monica: "Oh, what are we gonna do? I don't wanna see her."

Phoebe: "Ugh, let's just cut her out ... Just ignore her calls and dodge her 'til she gets the point."

Monica: "Oh, I guess we could try that, but ... it seems so harsh! (*to Chandler*) Have you ever done that?"

Chandler: "No, had it done to me though. Feels good."

From *Friends*[1]

The way she packs her own GMO-free lunches when she
    meets you and the kids at McDonald's.

The way she tongue-kisses her dog.

The way she texts *your* when she means *you're*.

The way the air freshener in her kitchen makes your sinuses
    twitch.

The way she keeps asking you to run 5K races with her.

The way she drinks decaf coffee at 8:00 a.m.

Whatever the reason, it's just time. It's time to break up.

As with romantic dating relationships, mommy breakups get harder the longer you've been together, the further you've gone, the more bases you've rounded.

At first base, the relationship can just naturally peter out as an activity wraps up and your schedules change. Or you can start standing on the other side of the soccer field until she gets the hint. A wayward toddler is also handy at this point. If the mom in question sidles over to strike up another conversation about her heirloom tomatoes, simply let the little one loose, then throw an apologetic look over your shoulder as you chase Baby Inara off the field. You can also plant the idea in your potty-training daughter's mind that she needs to go tee-tee, then spend the remainder of the game in the bathroom with her, scraping soggy toilet paper off her rear and trying to find a soap dispenser that works. Problem solved.

If you've already made it to second or third base, you have some options. Start with busy mode. You're just too busy, which is true. You have a limited amount of time for playdates, so they have to be fairly spectacular to warrant donning actual pants, jimmying kids into sticky five-point harnesses, and risking wood-chip splinters between your toes at the park. If the friend keeps calling, then you might have to throw your kid under the bus. "Spock is really struggling with sharing. For the safety of your child, we're going to have to cool things off a bit. Don't call us. We'll call you."

Here are some seasonal excuses that should give you a pass and keep you friend-free year-round:

Fall

1. We're still adjusting to the new school schedule.
2. We're still adjusting to the time change.
3. My child is very sensitive and we're holding a funeral for each leaf that falls.
4. Who are you? I got hit in the head by a pumpkin.

5. I'm lost in a corn maze.
6. We have a stuffing and pumpkin pie hangover.
7. Allergies.

Winter

1. It's taking longer than we thought to find the perfect Christmas tree.
2. We have the flu/bronchitis/bad cold/green boogers oozing amoeba-like from nostril to mouth in a steady stream.
3. We have a big family. One kid got the flu in December and we've been passing it around for two months.
4. Seasonal depression.
5. Valentine's Day depression.
6. I'm not talking to anyone until after January, when everyone finally shuts up about resolutions and realizes that they aren't going to the gym, they aren't giving up chocolate, and they can't read the whole Bible in one month.
7. Allergies.

Spring

1. We're packing for spring break.
2. We're on spring break.
3. We're unpacking from spring break.
4. We've given up playdates for Lent.
5. We're shopping for teacher appreciation week.
6. Allergies.
7. Allergies.

Summer

1. Oh, oops, did I not tell you which pool to go to? I was in the water and couldn't check my phone.
2. I dropped my phone in the pool.
3. We rented an RV and are touring all the national parks.
4. We went camping and I was mauled by a family of bears.

5. Don't invite us. My kids pee in the pool.
6. I suffer from reverse seasonal depression. I'm angry when I'm sweaty. (Uh, this one is actually true for me. I could write a whole book on this.)
7. Mosquitoes.

Vomit is a great excuse too. Any season, any time, just mention that someone vomited and no one will want to play with you. Heck, I don't even like the idea that we're connected through the internet if you've just puked. You can cancel any date, guilt-free, no questions asked, if you just text your friend that someone barfed.

I'm pretty lax about germs. You have to be if you have more than one kid and ever want to leave the house and see other humans. You have a cold? Fine, we just won't mouth kiss. Your kid has a low-grade fever? Meh, let's risk it and just lube up with hand sanitizer. Your baby barfed last week? Ugh, let's give it another three weeks just to be safe. Don't breathe on me. Full body shudder.

> Your baby barfed last week?
> ... Don't breathe on me. Full body shudder.

I had one friend whom I truly liked. I still miss her. We'd made it to third base and it was working great for both of us. We really liked each other, but our parenting styles were different. Which is fine. Unless she felt the need to instruct me and criticize. Which she did.

When we adopted our daughter, and all our poop hit a massive fan, things got messy. Daily life got hard. The screaming. So much screaming. (My daughter, not me—I became an Automaton droid from stuffing all the feelings deep, deep way down inside where they wouldn't shoot flames out my eyeballs.) So many behaviors erupting out of our traumatized little girl. I quickly learned about my own inadequacies to parent a child from a hard place, and all of us were just a mess.

We needed to be around safe people. We needed friends who wouldn't judge, wouldn't lecture, people who would just love us as we learned to love each other. So I needed a break from my critical third-base friend. At that point in our relationship, our kids didn't have any shared activities, so we just phased out. We didn't have a disagreement, and we ended gradually and peacefully. Over time, we just both stopped calling. I still think about her and wonder if I should reach out or just leave things as they are.

The Phases of a Phaseout

So, obviously, I don't really recommend that you lie to your friends about being mauled by a family of bears when things aren't working out between you. Tempting, but no. Actually, I'm a pretty direct person, but sometimes in the earlier stages of a friendship, you don't necessarily need a huge explanation for why things wind down. You don't need a come-to-Jesus moment because there isn't any real offense. It could simply be lack of shared interests, incompatibility in parenting styles, or opposite schedules. Things just … fizzle, and often it works both ways. With Critical Mom, yes, I stopped initiating with her, but she wasn't calling me either. My life got crazy and we just lost touch.

When you're the one doing the phasing out, you're aware of what's going on. But what happens when you don't know if you're being phased out or if she's just really busy? You're not close enough (or brave enough) to confront your friend openly. (There's a whole other chapter on that next, filled with fluffy rabbits and rainbows.) But the gap is widening like a short shirt with a stretched out pair of skinny jeans, and you don't know whether to hike 'em back up over your muffin top or just change pants.

It can leave you feeling neurotic and like, "What, did I forget to wear deodorant? What did I do?" And part of us wants to find out and part of us doesn't want the sweatiness that goes along with talking about it. This relational uncertainty goes through three phases.

Phase One: Mull over the history of the friendship. Is it worth trying to keep? Has this only ever been about killing time during ballet lessons? Is this friendship based solely on a couple of finger painting classes or because one time you forgot your smartphone at a bounce house birthday party and had to make small talk with the person standing next to you? Or is there something there? Remember the time she skipped her pilates class when you got sick and needed someone to pick up your kids at preschool? What about that afternoon when you discovered you could both still do the splits and you couldn't quit laughing?

I have a hard time letting go, so when a relationship is winding down, my first instinct is to try to bring us back together. I'm learning to evaluate the relationship before I try to force something that isn't there. Is it a relationship of convenience or possibly a lifelong friendship? There's nothing wrong with the former, and we don't have to force all of those to be the latter.

Phase Two (may take months): Issue light and nonthreatening invitations to get together. Evaluate her response. Does she only text or Facebook, but avoid meeting in person? Do you hear *of* her more than you hear *from* her? Ask her what she's working on, let her know you miss her, and give her space to see what she says. Maybe she's just busy with crazy life stuff and is desperately pining for you.

Phase Three: Suss out where you stand with her and dial back your emotional involvement if necessary. Maybe your relationship will be a dorky wave across the grocery store or maybe you'll get together a couple times a year to catch up.

I have several friends whom I love, but our lives just don't intersect anymore. We text once in a while and might see each other at a group event, but our one-on-one days are over because our kids are older and in separate activities. I'll always cherish the time we had together.

For other friends, maybe a phase-out leaves you ducking behind a display of canned goods and avoiding direct line of sight. Just be you, hold your head high, and smile like you mean it. And try to mean it.

If you've been recently phased out or had to phase someone out, persevere, woman, persevere. And if you're a little frustrated and put out by a particularly weird mama, may I speak for the weirdos? I am a full-fledged, socially awkward weirdo, and we are worth the investment. I'm sorry for that time I made a sci-fi reference when everyone else was talking about *The Bachelor*. I'm sorry for snort laughing when we went to the movies together. I'm sorry for correcting you when you mixed up Congo and the Democratic Republic of Congo. I'm sorry for not knowing who Adele was. Hug? Please don't phase me out. I may be weird, but I'm so flipping loyal. And I'll create a safe environment in which you also can snort laugh. Feel free.

Sadly, I am the mom that is phased out . . . often. There are special women out there who will make it to second base, and maybe even to third, but it is the really special mom who will become the fourth-baser. Why, you ask? What is wrong with her? (Other than having the same insecurities as many other moms, I, too, am a bit socially awkward, and I do love a good *Star Wars* reference.) She has a special needs kid. Yep, my kid is weird, and he laughs when he shouldn't, and he talks like an adult, and can melt down like no one's business, but he is smart and he is funny, and gives the best hugs when you are finally accepted. Perhaps there are moms out there who can help me understand why it is we are left in the lurch so often? Is it too uncomfortable? Are you afraid the autism will rub off onto your kid? Because it won't, I promise. Is it me? I think it would be easier to take, if it were me, and not my kid, because he can't help himself. Mom relationships are hard, even harder when special needs are involved, but I promise you this: they are so worth the extra effort! — *Mary T.*

Notes

1. "The One With Ross's Tan," *Friends*, National Broadcasting Company, aired October 9, 2003.

CHAPTER 27

Breaking Up Is Hard to Do:
The Confrontation

French Soldier: "I don't want to talk to you no more, you empty-headed animal food trough wiper. I fart in your general direction. Your mother was a hamster and your father smelt of elderberries." From *Monty Python and the Holy Grail*[1]

I know I promised you fluffy rabbits and rainbows. Um, if I could attach a multicolored Peeps smorgasbord to this book as kind of a gift-with-purchase, I would. But for realsies, we cannot phase out our fourth-basers. It's in the code. No phasing out of super close friends. That's just really cruel and lame. If you've shared deep stuff and need to break it off, that's exactly what it is. It's a break. A painful, sharp, fracture and it might take more than six weeks in a cast to heal. This is the scary part. We allow someone into our life, and when it breaks, it's excruciating.

For those of you who have to break up with fourth-basers,

yowza. Just yowch. I don't know if she keeps crashing your dates with your husband, showing up at your house late at night, or tried to taser one of your kids, but it must be bad. Fourthers are not easy to come by, and they're painful to lose.

And if you're on the receiving end? Someone who's seen the real you and says no … it's horrible. And you wasted a whole kid-free night on her too. And what about when you run into your former mom date at the park with—*gasp*—another mom? And her stroller is better than yours and she's wearing a baby like a champ and whips out her fancy stainless steel monogrammed water bottle while you're taking drags off your daughter's sippy cup from two days ago? Ouch. Refrain from whacking her with your overstuffed diaper bag. Now is a good time to pull out your phone. She doesn't need to know you're playing Flappy Bird. You could be texting your hot new mom date. Cuz she's out there. Waiting for you.

If you've been dumped, I prescribe chocolate frosting right out of the can and Nerds Rope. (See chapter 29 for more cathartic recipes.) Wallow, baby.

The single most devastating question I've ever asked on my blog was the following: "So, ladies, I have to know. What are your worst breakup stories?" In my naïveté, I thought I'd hear a few awkward stories. Never did I imagine that my comment section would fill with story after story of pain and loss. The battles were intense, and they were bloody. Scarred and shell-shocked women vowed never to venture into relationships again, and I sat at my computer and cried.

Although many moms were the victims of awkward phaseouts, the bloodiest breakups involved heartbreaking betrayal. As Commander Adama says in *Battlestar Galactica*,

> It's interesting. Betrayal has such a powerful grip on the mind. It's almost like a python. It can squeeze out all other thought, suffocate all other emotion until everything is dead except for the rage. I'm not talking about anger; I'm talking about rage. I can feel it. Right here, like it's gonna burst. I feel like I want to scream.[2]

You don't have to be fighting killer robots to know how he feels.

I had a particularly difficult breakup last year with a fourth-base friend. We knew each other for fifteen years. Her husband hired my husband and we moved from Baltimore to Milwaukee for this dream job and dream community. Eleven months later, the day after I returned from my mother's funeral, her husband laid mine off. And said God told him to. Did I mention we went to the same church? And that we rented their first-floor apartment? AWKWARD. But it gets worse. The promise of a year of health insurance was reneged. I had to quit my job at our church due to MAJOR conflicts. Flew to Pittsburgh for a "vacation" with the in-laws. Had emergency surgery. The day after I came home from the hospital, the girl calls me, doesn't ask how I am at all, then lays into me about why I left the church and how I have a problem with authority, and she talked to other people who loved us who agreed. For forty-five minutes this went on. I politely thanked her for her concern and acknowledged it couldn't have been easy to say to me. We never spoke again. We moved out a month later and have never heard from them since. The irony? She came to our residential ministry, homeless, those fifteen years ago, having left another outreach due to her problems with the leadership. I was the women's intake coordinator. I was the one who extended compassion, didn't doubt her perspective, and allowed her to MOVE INTO OUR COMMUNITY. Did that ever bite me in the end. — *Tammy P.*

Sometimes breakups with friends can hurt as badly as romantic breakups.

My breakup was one of the most painful things I've ever been through, since we were fourth-basers for over ten years. We are still friends (complete with the "post breakup hugs" — ha!), but it's just taken a different direction to where we don't spend the time together we used to and we don't go as deep into each other's lives. The phases I went through were EXACTLY like a guy/girl breakup. During her "I'm dumping you" speech, I was sobbing so hard I couldn't speak (which feels completely pathetic after the fact) and then I basically stayed locked up in my house for a week — didn't even shower! God has made a lot of beautiful things out of a really hard situation (such as opening my eyes to many other third- and fourth-basers already in my life that I didn't value as much as I should!), but I really wish I could have learned the lessons without so much pain. I think my greatest lesson in this is that God didn't really intend for us to have one person we put so much weight in that we are completely devastated when they disappoint us. We're going to be disappointed with all people at some point because they aren't God. I'm probably more careful than I need to be and sometimes I freak out that I have shared too much and then the person is going to feel awkward the next time we see each other! Mostly, though, I have found that they are more accepting than I thought they would be and I need to stop being so skeptical. I think it's important to know someone well enough that they've passed all of your "safe friend" tests, though, before sharing things that are really intimate. Some people aren't ever going to pass those, but I've learned to be okay with that and keep them at a certain distance. It's definitely a delicate balance! — *Stephanie E.*

Sometimes breakups happen due to betrayal, and sometimes it's because of unfulfilled expectations. Every person, including you, has a set of friendship expectations, some of which are plain and accepted everywhere (like kindness, loyalty, reciprocity), and some quirky ones which you guys didn't realize were there until one of you bumped up against them, like the following:

- I live out of town and have a busy career and not much energy for people interaction. I don't have time or energy for you other than our once or twice a year face-to-face visits.
- I will be a great friend to you while I live in the same town. Once I leave, I won't keep up the friendship anymore because I value face-to-face friends the most.
- I need to see you every week, but I will accept when you are busy.
- I will be a good friend while we are in similar circumstances (office, school, church, small group, child's activities).
- I will be a good friend because, even though you are very different from me, we are family and I will be seeing you a lot.
- I will be a good friend when I want something from you or want to prove something to you (ouch, but true).
- I will be a good friend as long as you let me cut you down (ouch again).
- I want to be a good friend but life is crazy so let's catch up once in a while and always believe the best of each other. And let's laugh. A lot.

Everyone has or establishes friendship rules, and the best friendships are where the friends are able to mostly play by each other's rules without getting angry or resentful. Sometimes a friend just can't live up to your quirky friendship rules. And sometimes you can't live up to hers. What then?

Face It

Aren't we all a bit conflict avoidant? I mean, is anyone just jonesing to have hard, sweaty-pitted conversations? I think most of us would rather skip it. But sometimes for our own sake and sanity we need to confront, if only to seek some resolution.

The breakup stories I read got me thinking about how we can

learn to confront with kindness. Some people are really good at it and can handle it like healthy adults. If you're like me, you get really shaky and sick and can't eat and break out in hives. Super fun. Confrontation can be freaky and terrible, but it is part of life, so what are some things we can do to survive it and maybe even come out on the other side with our momlationships intact?

I am not a relational dynamo, and I don't always get this stuff right. But here are some things that I practice and that I'm learning.

Get Humble

First, get humble. Seriously, before you talk to anyone about an issue, get by yourself, get quiet, and think about whether or not any part of the issue is coming from you. Maybe not all of it. But is there anything you've done that you need to own and apologize for? When you talk to your friend, start there. Open the conversation with a humble apology about your part of it.

When I know I need to talk with someone, I spend time contemplating my own ocular plank issues. Matthew 7:3–5 says,

> Why is it that you see the dust in your brother's or sister's eye, but you can't see what is in your own eye? Don't ignore the wooden plank in your eye, while you criticize the speck of sawdust in your [mom date's] eyelashes. That type of criticism and judgment is a sham! Remove the plank from your own eye, and then perhaps you will be able to see clearly how to help your [mom date] flush out [her] sawdust. (*Voice*)

My husband is fabulous at helping me with this. He risks me devouring him like Smaug the dragon, but he's Bilbo Baggins and stands up to my fire-breathing ways. He always, always, forces me to see the other person's side, and I both hate and love him for this.

Ask Questions and Listen

Second, ask questions. Listen to what she has to say, and remember point number one, get humble. I tend to want to defend myself, shoot back my opinion, and explain my side. I try to remind myself to Let. Her. Talk.

Two years ago, an elderly woman and a woman about my age came up to me in the grocery store. They accused me of slamming into the older woman and were very irate. The senior citizen got up in my face and accused me of rushing too fast, of not caring about anyone else. She took all her frustration with my generation and hurled it at me.

From my perspective, I had gently "ahemed" and "excuse me'd" several times to try to get around the two women having a conversation in the middle of the row. I was strung out in exhaustion from a demanding two-year-old who hated me and screamed at and hit me. While my husband kept the kids in the car, I ran into the store for five minutes of buying the essentials. When the women didn't hear me again and again, I finally as carefully as I could inched past them trying not to disturb them.

But. As this older woman launched at me while her friend stood nearby as backup, the Holy Spirit must've sat on my own, less-than-stellar personality and taken up the reins. What came out of my mouth was compassion. I listened and I repeated back to her how I'd made her feel, startled and bumped in the middle of her conversation. She felt like I didn't care about her, like I didn't respect her, like I was rushing too quickly to take the time to go around. And I was sorry. Somewhere in my listening to what she had to say, I broke. My circumstances stayed the same. My reasons and my "side" still stayed the same, but my compassion for her perspective overwhelmed my need to win, to be right. This was a stranger, but listening and hearing her side and feeling compassion is even more effective with friends.

Fight Fairly

Third, don't take cheap shots. Fight fairly. Avoid "always," "never," and "should." You *should always never* say those words. Avoid bringing other people into the mix. Nothing drives me crazier than when someone tries to bring other people into the conflict. "We've all been talking, and this is how we all feel." Speak for yourself, and don't try to create an army of additional people who all agree with you. If other people have the same issue, then they need to bring it up with her. Don't be a spokesperson for a group of people. That just exposes your gossip.

Make it about you. Personalize it. *Sometimes I feel like this when you do that. Because of my issues with blah, I often feel this when you do this thing.*

Time It

Fourth, pick the right timing. Right after she finds out she has melanoma is not the right timing. Remember that at one point you loved this person.

Be Graciously Honest

Fifth, be honest. I don't mean to use honesty harshly. Don't eviscerate her with honesty. But be honest with her about what's going on and how you feel. Respectfully honest. Graciously honest.

I pray a lot for the right timing and the right words. I'm so fallible, so messy, and I have to ask God into my conflicts, to guide me and protect my friend, because without him, I'll muck up everything.

At my sister-in-law's rehearsal dinner, lovely people gave incredibly insightful and touching toasts. (Unlike her brother and myself, whose toast may or may not have involved a medley, props, jazz hands, and the words "take off your top.") One wise friend talked about the power of being wrong.

Learn how to be wrong.[3] This is incredible advice for every relationship, whether it's in a marriage, in a friendship, with an employer, or in parenting. We're all wrong from time to time, some of us more than others, and it's how we handle the being wrong that matters.

Learn how to be wrong.

First, you have to recognize when you're wrong. For me, this usually happens halfway through the sentence that I'm belligerently spewing with every confidently locked bone in my body. *Oh snap. I'm wrong. What do I do? That thing they said that I interrupted with the force of my brilliant opinion just registered in my brain and they're right oh bleep oh bleep oh bleep.*

At that point you have some options.

Option One

Go for broke. They don't know that you know that they're right. Just keep digging your own grave until you burrow through the earth's core, pop out on the other side of the world, and catch the red-eye home.

Option Two

Stop and get humble. *Oh! Whoops, you're right, I'm wrong, my bad, thanks for that, I needed to hear that, I didn't know.* If you've already started digging, take a deep breath, say you're sorry, and ask them to forgive you. This one's hard, but leads to deeper relationships. The more you humble yourself and admit you're wrong, the easier it is to do it. And it keeps people from walking on eggshells around you, being afraid of you, writing you off as a moron, or getting mad.

Everyone is wrong some of the time. And humility is a little bit sexy. A lot sexy. When you're willing to admit you don't have a total grasp on everything there is to know in the universe, you allow space for others to come into your world and exist around you in harmony.

There's freedom in learning to be wrong. You give the people around you permission to be right. You become approachable. If I think about the people I admire most, they're the humble ones, the truly teachable people who are not afraid to admit when they're wrong or don't know something.

There's freedom in learning to be wrong. You give
the people around you permission to be right.

I'm learning to be wrong in my marriage, and that is no easy
deal for me. I'm hardwired to want to tell my husband how it is.
I'm also learning to be wrong in my parenting and to humble
myself before my kids. I hope they learn that if Mommy can do
it, so can they.

> My story is a bit different . . . more of a cautionary tale. I was
> the horrible friend: I broke up with a great friend a few years
> ago because I could not set boundaries for myself or say no,
> so if I did not want to hang out or talk on the phone, instead
> of saying how I honestly felt, I kept it all inside and just went
> along with whatever was initiated. I inevitably got angry
> and frustrated, felt smothered, and broke it off. I was cruel,
> abrupt, and spineless. After a few months went by, I missed
> my friend. I also got a sobering view of what the real issue
> was . . . it was me. I asked for forgiveness and my friend
> forgave me. Slowly our relationship was rebuilt and she
> has become my best friend. Her forgiveness still astounds
> and impacts me (often to tears) and allows me to be more
> forgiving to others. — *Candace M.*

We're all wrong sometimes. Whether we're the primary
person at fault or part of the problem, often somewhere in the
entanglement we'll find at least a little of our own junk for which
we can take responsibility.

Sometimes despite our best efforts, the relationship is over.
You rounded the bases together. You spent hours and hours sharing your lives. But for The Reason, whatever it is, it's over. If
you're early in your base rounding, this is a natural course of life
and probably simply involves a schedule change or a move. Or

maybe you just aren't clicking, but there are no hard feelings, no shared vulnerability to make the separation painful.

If you're further along, it's deeper, it's rougher, and it hurts more. No matter how things shake out, own your mistakes, ask for forgiveness, and be gracious.

"If it is possible, as far as it depends on you, live at peace with everyone" (Romans 12:18). As far as it depends on you. Do everything you can to live peaceably, but if the relationship is becoming poisonous, if she's manipulating and lying and a total sociopath and you wake up and find yourself on a crazy train headed toward a mountain with no tunnel and you've tried talking with her and the relationship is oozing into all aspects of your life, then yeah, time to come up for that breather, get healthy, and heal. Forgiveness doesn't always mean togetherness. Sometimes walking away from a relationship is the only way to find peace.

Forgiveness doesn't always mean togetherness.

And finding peace after a breakup ... well, that can be a road.

Notes

1. *Monty Python and the Holy Grail*, directed by Terry Gilliam and Terry Jones, Michael White Productions, 1975.

2. "Home: Part 1," *Battlestar Galactica*, R&D TV, aired August 19, 2005.

3. Thank you, Julie Theis, for sharing this wise advice!

‖ CHAPTER 28 ‖

When You Want to Mow Her Down with Your Minivan

Mrs. White: "I hated her so much ... flames ... on the side of my face."

From *Clue*[1]

Flames. On the side of your face. Homicidal rage. She's sliced you to the core of your very being and you want payback.

Some of us respond to conflict with anger and indignation. Or if you're like me, you're just really, really sad and neurotic. Occasionally, something will push me over the edge into actual anger, but usually when I'm dealing with a friend, I just feel devastated. Rather than revving up my minivan, I want to crawl in a hole and race around on a gerbil wheel of regret. I grieve my friends, and I think through every single thing I could've done differently and every way I feel misunderstood.

One time I really liked another girl and we spent hours and hours together. I opened up and shared large chunks of my life with her, but she didn't really share much back. She talked negatively about a lot of other girls we knew, and as I listened to her, I warned myself that at some point, she'd do the same to me. Sure enough, a few months later, she abruptly stopped talking to me. I asked her if anything was wrong, and she assured me that we were fine. Another friend told me what she'd been saying about me, things that were untrue and hurtful. I learned to beware the super good listener who soaks up all your details but doesn't reciprocate. Vulnerability is a two-way street.

I tend to overthink things and while I think of this breakup often and the details that got us there, I doubt the other mom wonders at all. For a while it seemed great. We liked the same books and could try on shoes for an hour both knowing we did not intend to buy a single pair. Life started happening, and our lives were not aligning as easily anymore. We weren't raising our children the same, our husbands got along but weren't going to be best friends, and we were hanging out with other friends more often than each other. I went through a really bad few months where I was Judgy McJudgerson and I really didn't like people during that time. I would roll my eyes at harmless Facebook posts and Twitter updates by this mom and hated myself for it. I was being petty and jealous and condemning all at once, but all in my head. I let all of the negativity eat me up and I pushed this mom away, not that there was a lot of trying on her end (busy lives and all), but I was most definitely not trying. I found myself bringing her "faults" up to other friends and my husband and gossiping and being so ugly and sinful. I hated myself even more. I finally just had to pray a lot and separate myself from her completely. Like I said, though, I don't think she's really noticed it was intentional so much as our lives got busier and we just naturally grew apart. I am nice and civil now when we run into each other, but I can't be invested the way I was before. — Kim T.

After one difficult breakup I became scared of my phone. My hands shook and I felt paralyzed with indecision about what to do. I was like my parents' Chihuahua, Pebbles, who shakes so hard during thunderstorms that she has to wear a tight little security jacket. I couldn't turn on my phone, had trouble eating, and just sat in a room tormenting myself with every word of the conflict.

Over the years, I have learned a few things from my breakups, from the less invasive parting-of-ways to the excruciating amputations. Thankfully, I've been able to work through most of the difficulties I've had with other moms, savoring their forgiveness of my junk and extending grace to them for theirs. Of the few relationships where we just couldn't work it out, here are a few things that helped me cope and come out on the other side.

Write It Down

First, write it all down. Open up a Word document or grab a journal. Write out the whole bloody scenario like you're making a record for future generations to see the ins and outs and whys. Draft your bilious memoirs. Write her a letter about how she's rendered you a shell of a woman. Tell her how much you wish you could pull her hair and spit in her coffee. Write letters to all your friends. Create an entire letter-writing campaign for why things went down the way they did and how you were wronged.

Also write down what you did, anything you caused, all the ways you contributed to the issue, even if you have to really scrape to come up with anything because of how amazing and perfect you were through the whole thing. Think of anything you could've done differently. Write a tome. Use bullets (just to be clear, that's bullet points, not actual bullets) if you hate writing. Make lists. Pour it all out.

And I think you know what's coming. Don't send any of it. Store it in a box, delete it, roast s'mores over the fire pit of all your grief, or rip each piece into tiny pieces. Purge all your emotions and thoughts and use your words to wrap your head around everything that happened.

One time my husband wrote a scathing letter to the mortgage company that shafted us, just as a catharsis. He didn't send it, but the exercise helped to purge his brain of the ugly thoughts he had. He really wanted to go down there and throw things and make threats, and the secret letter helped him stop clenching whenever their name came up and probably saved us from having to leave town.

When I had a difficult misunderstanding with another mom and felt unfairly thrown under the proverbial bus, I wrote down everything, from start to finish, exactly as it had played out. The process of doing that helped me organize everything that had happened and get my head on straight.

Tell God Everything

Second, scream at God. Tell him everything. Tell him you want vengeance. Don't make it pretty. Don't try to sound like a good person. He knows what's really going on, so just show him all your wounds.

Sometimes I gross myself out when I have all these terrible, evil, horrific thoughts and feelings, and then I go to pray and I'm all,

> Dear Lord, thank you for the opportunity to love this person *(Why am I trying to spin this for God's benefit? Lies!)*
>
> and for your love, gracious, loving, Lord *('Cuz I'm so into the love in this fine moment).*
>
> Oh, Lord, how you love us *(Really, really, scraping here).*
>
> Please be with her *(BE with her? BE with her? What does that even mean?!?).*
>
> Help me to forgive her *(I'm going to need a lot more help than I even know).*
>
> In Jesus' name *(Do I even understand how powerful that is?),*
>
> Amen *(Nailed it).*

In the Bible, I see people donning sackcloth and ashes, tearing their clothing apart, lamenting. I'm not sure how we ended up with our bland, passive practice of throwing out altruisms about how "God's got this," and "Everything happens for a reason," as if showing emotion equates to showing doubt.

When we get upset, we aren't necessarily doubting God's sovereignty. We're showing our trust in his love. Our loving God is on the throne, and that should give us more permission to let it all out. He's on the *throne*. He isn't going to freak out, like "Oh, dang, she's really upset. I don't know how to handle that." He's powerful and can handle my emotion. He can handle it when I totally fall apart, and I'm safe in his arms.

So fall apart.

I don't have a pretty, quiet, subdued relationship with God. When my heart hurts, I let him know about it. I like to think that then we full-frontal hug it out. He rescues us and delights in us.

> In my distress I called to the LORD;
>> I cried to my God for help.
> From his temple he heard my voice;
>> my cry came before him, into his ears …
> He parted the heavens and came down …
> He reached down from on high and took hold of me;
>> he drew me out of deep waters.
> He rescued me from my powerful enemy …
> They confronted me in the day of my disaster,
>> but the LORD was my support.
> He brought me out into a spacious place;
>> he rescued me because he delighted in me.
>> PSALM 18:6, 9A, 16–17A, 18–19

I'm a high-functioning claustrophobic person. I don't end up in the corner rocking myself or anything, but elevators freak me out and I try to avoid them whenever possible. I always need to feel like I have a way out. My husband knows this about me and makes sure to give me the seat facing the door in a crowded restaurant. I act like John Cusack in *Grosse Pointe Blank* and was probably a professional assassin in another life.

When I feel like people misunderstand me and I have relational difficulty, I can feel squeezed, trapped. I love how this psalm says that God comes down and brings me into a spacious place. I have written at the top of this page in my Bible S P A C I O U S!

When we're squeezed and trapped and fall apart, he gets us out in the open where we can breathe again.

Get Quiet

The third thing is the hardest one, especially for external processors, those of us who need to talk everything out with everyone around them. What I'm about to say I do not say lightly. This is one of the most important and most difficult things for me to do after I've been hurt. It's easy to suggest, but very difficult to execute.

Get quiet.

It sounds so reasonable and effortless. For those of us who are talkers, it's the hardest thing in the universe. When I'm hurt, I want to tell everyone about it, about how she lied and destroyed me. I want to explain myself, to make sure everyone knows my side.

But I can't. I would just come off sounding defensive and gossipy. No matter how much I feel like roadkill smooshed on the grill of her Semi of Fury, I try to talk God's ear off about it and stay quiet with everyone else.

When I went through a rough breakup, I had a friend share a verse from the Psalms that released me to have total freedom from the responsibility of my reputation. She knew none of the details of my circumstances, because I was staying true to "get quiet," but she felt prompted to tell me,

> In my integrity you uphold me
> and set me in your presence forever.
> PSALM 41:12 (NIV 1984)

God upholds our integrity. We don't have to try to defend it ourselves. Oh.

Does this sound familiar to you?

> When one of them comes to see me,
>   [s]he speaks falsely, while [her] heart gathers slander;
>   then [s]he goes out and spreads it around.
> All my enemies whisper together against me;
>   they imagine the worst for me . . .
> Even my close friend,
>   someone I trusted,
> one who shared my bread,
>   has turned against me.

PSALM 41:6–7, 9

If that's happened to you, I'm just, *sigh*, I'm just so sorry. Sometimes I feel like I need to suck on a tube of Preparation H to keep my lips tight and not flapping about all the injustice and misrepresentation. But no matter how frustrated I feel about a situation, I try to focus on my own junk and not share hers with the world.

The rancid cherry on top of the heartache and sense of loss after a breakup is often the feeling that people in the world think badly of you, or worse, are saying it, and to lots of people. I can start to feel like the whole world is talking about how awful I am and become this paranoid person who definitely wants to stay inside and eschew human beings for the rest of my life. But I'm learning to let God uphold my integrity, lay down my insecurities, and try to move forward filled with love, not bitterness.

The other thing I tell myself is that it isn't about me. Most of life isn't about me, and most people don't live their lives thinking about me all the time. When I see someone making a weird eyeball at me from across the preschool classroom, it's probably just a bad contact lens and not because she heard about that thing that went down between me and that person at that time on that one day then.

The following verse keeps me from engaging in a lot of the exchanges on social media. Well, this verse and the fact that I can't handle arguing. During the last presidential election, I caught myself holding my sides and rocking during the debates.

> Don't have anything to do with foolish and stupid arguments, because you know they produce quarrels. And the Lord's servant must not be quarrelsome but must be kind to everyone, able to teach, not resentful.
>
> 2 TIMOTHY 2:23–24

(Of course not all arguments are foolish and stupid ... but maybe some of them are?)

I think most of us would agree that we want to raise our kids to be kind. I pray that they'll be kind to their peers and kind to each other. So far, I'm failing miserably with that last part, but at least we're having conversations about treating each other with kindness. Part of raising kind kids is for us to model kindness. No matter what kind of disagreement or difficulty arises between us as mothers, I hope that we will disagree kindly and respectfully. Our relationships aren't always going to work out. We cannot get along with every single woman in our lives. But even in the not working out, we can show gentleness and humility.

And I believe, with time and Jesus, our hearts can heal.

Notes

1. *Clue*, directed by Jonathan Lynn, Paramount Pictures, 1985.

How To Make Mojo
3 cups of awesome
6 tablespoons of confidence

Bring to a boil
Add salt

RECIPES

‖ CHAPTER 29 ‖

How to Get Your Mojo Back

Bob Wiley: "Hi, I'm Bob. Would you knock me out, please?
Just hit me in the face."   From *What About Bob?*[1]

You'll never love another.

She's gone, she done you wrong, and you're singing your song.
You've lost that lovin' feelin'.

Dr. Evil stole your mojo and time machined it to the '60s.

Just like a romantic breakup, sometimes we need chocolate,
wine, or a big bowl of ice cream. Or
all three on a rotation basis. About
now we should probably discuss
the appropriate movie, chocolate,
and ice cream pairings, based on
the level of betrayal and desire to
hurt her with your thoughts.

I also find comfort in reading

Via Twitter @UnexpectedMel

Elliott asked me if I had
a baby in my tummy.
"Why do you ask?" "Oh, it
looked like it, that round
part." Sigh. Food baby.
Tamales, worth it.

the Psalms when I'm upset, because David, the king who wrote a lot of them, spent a ton of time begging God to slay his enemies and make them pay. It's a little cathartic to read his words about his enemies, and frankly it's a relief to know that his rants are found in Scripture.

Here are several methods I employ to reclaim my mojo. Notice that all of them involve eating and none of them involve exercise. I did go through one season of relational strife when I trotted around the neighborhood every morning and talked to God about the whole darn mess. That just tells you how kerfloofy I was about it. When I have to resort to exercise to work something out, people, it must really be bad.

Mulling It Over

When you're mulling things over and replaying the breakup in your head over and over, you need mulled wine. If you don't drink wine, mulled cider is also excellent. Just go mull something. I went on some mom dates with a friend from eastern Europe who introduced me to mulled wine, and in Latvia at Christmastime, it's simmering over fires at the outdoor Christmas markets and smells lovely. There are many different ways to tweak this, but here's how I usually do it:

1. Pour a bottle of red wine (or cider) into a pot on the stove. I usually use whatever I have left from the last time I opened a bottle.
2. Add a couple of cinnamon sticks, a few cloves, a dollop of honey, and some peeled orange slices. I've also subbed out the honey for molasses or sorghum. Whatever you like.
3. Bring to a simmer for twentyish minutes. I like to get it going on the stove, then go tuck my kids in bed. It's ready when I come back.
4. Ladle into a mug and grip your neurotic hands around it.
5. Breathe in the fragrant steam, and breathe out your churning brain replays.

6. Stop mulling over the breakup and start sipping your mulled wine.

7. Mull over some Psalmage, and get King Davidy:

> Let the morning bring me word of your unfailing love,
>   for I have put my trust in you.
> Show me the way I should go,
>   for to you I entrust my life.
> Rescue me from my enemies, LORD,
>   for I hide myself in you.
>
> PSALM 143:8–9

8. Pair with warm apple pie, a gingersnap cookie, or a piece of fair-trade dark chocolate.

9. Movie suggestion: the BBC version of *Pride and Prejudice* with Colin Firth and Jennifer Ehle. It's six hours of delightful banter that will make you forget all about so-and-so and your Big Problems. It has to be the BBC version, because they capture all the humor from the book. Mr. Collins is presented in all his goofy, asinine splendor. Your problems could be worse. Your fortune could be entailed away and you could be pressured to marry an idiot.

Biting Your Tongue

When you're biting back your tongue and really want to pick up the phone and chew her out, go with spicy cocoa. Add as much cayenne as you need to burn off your taste buds and fully disable your vocal cords. Equal Exchange sells a delicious spicy cocoa, or you can make your own:

1. Put 2 tablespoons-ish of fair-trade cocoa powder in a bowl.
2. Heat up a cup of milk. (I use almond.)
3. While the milk is heating, sprinkle sugar, ground cinnamon, and cayenne pepper into the cocoa and mix it all together.
4. Stir it into the hot milk.

5. Add more sugar if you like it sweet, and add more cayenne pepper if you can still feel your tongue.

6. While your tongue is temporarily disarmed, read what Jesus' brother had to say about our tongues:

> With the tongue we praise our Lord and Father, and with it we curse human beings, who have been made in God's likeness. Out of the same mouth come praise and cursing. My brothers and sisters, this should not be.
>
> JAMES 3:9–10

7. If you like pain, drink this while munching on wasabi peas. I like it with popcorn and a glass of water, because I'm a wuss.

8. Movie suggestion: *Amelie*. It is impossible to think negative thoughts while watching this movie. *Amelie* makes me want to go hug the whole world. You will smile till your face hurts. And her pranks on the mean grocer are bound to provide you with intense satisfaction. (Do not watch this with your kids, because there are boobies.)

Crying Till It's Ugly

When you've cried till your throat hurts and your eyes sting, you need herbal tea. As a die-hard coffee drinker, this is hard for me to admit, but sometimes you just need tea. Even me. My tea recipe is a family secret, so get ready for this.

1. Boil water.

2. Grab a bag of chamomile or loose-leaf Rooibos. You can go with mate if you need a bang of caffeine along with the soothing quality of tea. (It's a South American tea that's kinda considered the coffee-lovers tea, I guess for those of us coffee-lovers who want to slum it with tea once in a while.)

3. When the teapot starts to whistle, use that opportunity to get out any last wailing in anguish.

4. Pour boiling water into a mug. (This is the secret step nobody knows about.)

5. As you dunk the bag or tea ball into the mug and the steam pricks your eyes and nose, have a tissue on hand to catch drips.

6. King David has got your back on this one. Nobody does misery like King David. When people say ridiculous things about women being more emotional than men, I think of King David, who penned some of the most beautiful, heart-wrenching words in all of literature.

> I am feeble and utterly crushed;
>   I groan in anguish of heart.
> All my longings lie open before you, Lord;
>   my sighing is not hidden from you.
> My heart pounds, my strength fails me;
>   even the light has gone from my eyes.
> My friends and companions avoid me because of my wounds;
>   my neighbors stay far away.
> Those who want to kill me set their traps,
>   those who would harm me talk of my ruin;
>   all day long they scheme and lie.
>
> PSALM 38:8–12

7. Ice cream tastes amazing with a sore throat. (Coconut ice or sorbet for my fellow diarrheal friends.) Alternate hot tea and cold ice cream until you're in a soothing emotional coma. It could be worse. You could be King David.

8. Movie suggestion: *You've Got Mail*. Meg Ryan at her adorablest. There's a lot of tea drinking in this movie, and coffee drinking, so it's an equal opportunity hot beverage movie. Oh, but the Shop Around the Corner will enchant you. You'll cry with Meg, and then you'll twirl. Make sure to twirl with her. It always helps. And use a real handkerchief.

Ranting Up a Sweat

When you've ranted to yourself so hard that you've worked up a sweat, replenish with a smoothie. Smoothies cool off my mouth, take down my overheated body temperature, and also give me a convenient brain freeze, rendering me unable to think any more about the problem.

1. Fill up the blender with spinach or kale.
2. Add a smooshie banana and frozen strawberries.
3. Add a strawberry or vanilla yogurt. (I use coconut faux yogurt.)
4. Splash orange juice on top of everything.
5. Take out any residual aggression on the "pulse" button. Die, pulse button, die!
6. Oh, King David, preach, brother, preach. His friends were running away from him in the street. There's something about his laments that just resonates with me, even though I've never had an army chase me around town and try to kill me.

> Because of all my enemies,
>   I am the utter contempt of my neighbors
> and an object of dread to my closest friends—
>   those who see me on the street flee from me.
> I am forgotten as though I were dead . . .
> But I trust in you, LORD;
>   I say, "You are my God."
> My times are in your hands;
>   deliver me from the hands of my enemies,
>   from those who pursue me . . .
> Let me not be put to shame, LORD,
>   for I have cried out to you;
> but let the wicked be put to shame
>   and be silent in the realm of the dead.
> Let their lying lips be silenced,
>   for with pride and contempt
>   they speak arrogantly against the righteous.
> How abundant are the good things
>   that you have stored up for those who fear you,
> that you bestow in the sight of all,
>   on those who take refuge in you.
> In the shelter of your presence you hide them
>   from all human intrigues;

you keep them safe in your dwelling
    from accusing tongues.

PSALM 31:11–12, 14–15, 17–20

7. I like to eat salty potato chips with my smoothies. The salt cuts the sweet and keeps me from feeling overly healthy with all the smoothie nutrients.
8. Movie suggestion: *Girls Just Wanna Have Fun*, because the part where they sabotage the nasty girl's party is hilarious; I mean, let's pray for them. This movie always makes me get up and dance, so stand on the sofa and go for it. Earn your spot on Dance TV.

Prayer of Blessing

Take enough time to heal, but not enough time to erect walls as high as the CN Tower. If you feel yourself morphing from mourning to hiding, it's time to get back out there and learn to love again.

So many of us walk around with open wounds. We don't know how to heal, and we carry these gaping holes in our hearts for years. I did.

Whenever I met someone with the same name as a person who hurt me, I internally flinched. You know that movie with Bill Murray and Andie MacDowell when they live the exact same day over and over? I had *Groundhog Day* of the brain, turning events over and over in my mind, trying to find a way to make the circumstances change.

One day I'd had enough. I finally decided that every time I caught myself stewing about the relationship, I'd stop and replace the thoughts with a prayer of blessing for the other person. Son of a bee sting, did I ever have to pray for her a lot.

But that was my journey out of my mental *Groundhog Day*. Stop. Catch myself. Pray for God to bless her, to encourage her, to lavish his love all over her. Dang it.

Even though the relationship is no less broken, my heart

has slowly healed. This is all Jesus' fault. He came here to earth and flip-flopped everything we knew about how to treat people, saying ridiculous things like, "You have heard that it was said, 'Love your neighbor and hate your enemy.' But I tell you, love your enemies and pray for those who persecute you" (Matthew 5:43–44).

Dang it. It really works. It isn't enough to make yourself stop thinking about someone. You have to replace those thoughts with something else, or you'll just keep swirling back to Crazy Town. Prayer Replacement Therapy. And not, "Lord help her see the error of her ways." Nope. That just enables me to feel morally superior. I have to pray blessings. Blessings for her as a mother, blessings for her kids. Blessings for her to feel loved and whole and beautiful.

Dang. It. And also, thank you, God, for helping me find a path to sanity.

Notes

1. *What About Bob?* directed by Frank Oz, Touchstone Pictures, 1991.

‖ CHAPTER 30 ‖

Screw Your Courage

Jason Nesmith: "Never give up. Never surrender."
From *Galaxy Quest*[1]

You twitch when another mom even smiles at you. You catch yourself planning escape strategies when you're standing near other moms. The room mom from your son's class invited you over to plan the Christmas party and you blacked out a little. You make final judgments about other women just by looking at them across the football field.

Other women look like enemies, and you've insulated yourself from close relationships. You're terrified of ever being hurt like that again.

You're an island.

Picture an island in your mind, a tropical one with palm trees or a desert one with cacti. The crystal blue water laps its sandy beaches and the gentle breezes keep the temperature perfect all year long. I don't know anyone who wouldn't want to visit an island. They are desirable in every way. There's only one big thing wrong with an island.

It's hard to get to. You need multiple modes of transportation to get to an island. You drive to an airport and get on a plane, or you drive, fly, then take a boat. At the very least, you drive, pay a toll, sit in traffic, and drive across a big bridge or ferry across. It's complicated.

Islands are all by themselves. They're glittering and gorgeous and all alone.

If you're an island, I'm swimming over. Ahoy.

After a bad breakup, finding the strength to get out there again and make friends requires crushing your inner cynic. When you've been hurt, either by unavoidable circumstances or by the surgical slices of a sociopath straight out of the movie *Heathers* (*Mean Girls* for anyone born after circa 1985), it's basic survival instinct to stay safely inside our mutant ninja turtle shells.

Via Twitter @UnexpectedMel

Me: I want to quit life and watch Doctor Who.

Hubs: I know. But what happens when Doctor Who is over?

Me: Shh.

Be brave. Not every woman on the planet is out to get you—maybe only half. Give yourself permission to take things slowly, but make yourself build a bridge off your island. Or at least buy a hovercraft.

After we've been hurt, and after we've healed, it's time to screw on our courage and get back out there.

Big-Girl Pants (BGPs)

My daughter Evie is probably the smartest person I know. When I talk to her, I can just see the little wheels turning in her head. She's always one step ahead, is one move up on me, and has a killer endgame. She loves planning and wants to stick to her plan no matter what.

Which is why I'm pretty sure when she was two, she plotted ahead of time to potty train herself on our road trip to the beach. I am not making this up.

In one day, she went from happily peeing all over herself to insisting that she put on BGPs and stop at every rest stop between our driveway and the sand dunes of the Atlantic. Our five-hour road trip became seven, and I didn't think we'd ever make it to vacation.

The best thing about diapers is not having to stop for toddler-sized bathroom breaks, and Evie relished her complete control of our minivan, because no one wants a urine-soaked car seat. That's yucky, even for us.

Each summer, Martha and I rent a house together and enjoy a week of fourth-base beachery with all our kiddos splashing around and our hubbies getting bromantic over sub sandwiches and shark sightings. The summer when Evie was two, our rental happened to have five million sets of stairs, with the bathroom on the top floor. We spent the week racing up the stairs carrying Evie to the potty, like some kind of horrendous training regimen for an Iron Man contest. And on the trip back, sure enough, we saw the inside of every gas station from Hilton Head Island to Atlanta, until forty minutes from home, when Alex and I finally told her we were done stopping and to just pee on herself. We're awesome parents like that. (And for the record, she held it like a boss.)

But good for Evie. When she decided to potty train, she got on it with a vengeance. Wearing BGPs takes work, and courage, because you have to listen to your body, assert yourself with everyone around you, and risk making a fool of yourself.

To the Sticking-Place

Evie's come a long way. Since that first beach trip in her BGPs, now she can go all day long, although she still can't resist the lure of an uncharted public bathroom. She's wearing her big-girl pants with confidence. And you can, too.

We all need to put on our BGPs and get courageous. I want my bravery on when my kids try to blow past bedtime, and I need it nice and tight when I'm scared of other women and don't want to talk to anyone because of the heart muscle memories of the previous pain.

"Screw your courage to the sticking-place" and start making eye contact with other moms again. Of course, Lady MacB said that to her husband when she was encouraging him to murder King Duncan, so if you're feeling murderous, maybe don't screw anything, least of all your courage.[2]

Big-girl pants, courage screwing, however you want to say it, we need to be brave. Here are two halves of the same story. Two moms, burned before and afraid to love again, met each other and had a decision to make. Would they risk their hearts again?

Part One: Jennifer's Story

During my early years of college, I had a friendship that was amazingly good and beautiful. We promised to stay friends forever, be in each other's weddings, have children who would grow up to be the best of friends like us because our friendship was that strong. Year three of our friendship brought about a drastic change. Suddenly, the promise of forever turned into avoidance, silence, and a terrible sadness. I was devastated and confused that an extraordinary friendship could end so coldly and abruptly, and with it the optimism that I would ever have a friendship like that again also died. I reminisced for twenty-four years hoping that she would come back, or I would find someone else.

The life of being a wife and stay-at-home mother to three children consumed all of my time and energy. My house was immaculate, the lawn perfectly manicured, and the cars were all showroom ready because I didn't take time to focus on friendships. I simply gave up.

Then two years ago, a casual acquaintance with another mom gave me a flicker of hope. We were both volunteer leaders of our girls' scout troop. I really enjoyed working with Mary Elizabeth and always had a great time; I knew there was more to her, but I wasn't sure she liked me.

An opportunity arose to take the girls in our troop to a concert. I ended up being one of the drivers and was anxious about who would ride with me. I was happy that Mary Elizabeth chose to be my navigator, and this would be the test to see if we could really be better friends. The ride down went very well, and we continued talking throughout the weekend about deeper topics. I was amazed at how different she was compared to the assumptions of her I had in my head. We were opposites in a lot of areas, but the differences were attractive because I could see how her friendship could grow those areas of weakness in my life.

My expectations were very high. I was waiting for the moment to surface where I knew the friendship could not go any deeper, and I would be proven right again that you only get one shot at that "once in a lifetime friend." We started an email correspondence, which led to deeper discussions and also a freedom to be more open. We spent more free time with each other, just having a great time talking or helping each other out with projects. My insecurities were quickly fading, and I was humbled beyond belief that God would give me a second opportunity at yet another incredible friendship. He used this new friend to mend the hurt of the past but also to show me that this one is even better.

I have never had a sister to compare the female friend dynamic to, but I know that I love and cherish Mary Elizabeth as if she were. I wandered around in the wilderness for a long time and gave up all hope of ever finding a close female friend. God used that time of solitude and loneliness to mend my heart and prepare it to be made whole again in his timing. She has given me back years of my life through happiness and laughter. I matter to someone outside of my family, and we have the best times being ourselves without our labels of mom and wife. There are no demands or expectations of one another, just mercy and grace. I thank God for her every day in my prayers, for his gracious and wonderful gift that has enriched my life! — *Jennifer G.*

Part Two: Mary Elizabeth's Story

I'd given up on having a best friend. In fact, I'd deliberately taken an oath saying that I'd have no more after losing my fifth best friend in ten years.

A few moved away. One stopped talking to me out of the blue, and I didn't find out till seven years later why. (It was a problem she was dealing with and nothing I had done.) In the aftermath of that failed friendship, though, I entered into another friendship that was founded on negativity and bitterness. I suppose it's no surprise then that it ended negatively and bitterly. And painfully.

I kept my oath for four lonely years and kept the people around me at first base. In the meantime, God used that time to heal some wounded places in my heart.

I worked with a great group of ladies for a scouting group. One day, we decided to take our girls on a road trip. I ended up riding along with the one leader I didn't know as well as the others, Jennifer, and we had four hours to get to know each other. I mean, we'd actually known each other for a couple of years, but as we both later admitted, we were each intimidated by the other person. However, we actually had to talk to each other beyond small talk, and it was one of those moments when you realize, "Hey, this person is cool. I need to know her better." We continued to get to know each other a little bit more as the months wore on.

That summer, she found out that I was a complete moron when it came to landscaping. This wasn't exactly hard to figure out. She took one look at my three acres and shook her head in disbelief and dismay. She is a landscaping genius, as well as a kind and generous person who takes pity on those in need, and she offered to help me.

It was in that experience that we realized the depth of the friendship we could create. I wasn't looking for a best friend; I'd given up on that, and so had she. But I'm so glad that God had other plans for us.

If this were a movie script, now would be the time where I'd say that it was smooth sailing thereafter, and everything was rainbows and butterflies. But this is real life, and we're real people, with issues, traumas, sin, and hidden places we are afraid to expose to the light. Here is the incredibly cool thing, though. We began to share those hidden places. We exposed them to the light. We shared our ugly places. Tentatively, slowly, with trepidation. And God gave us a bit of his grace and mercy so that we could be his light in each other's lives. Instead of judgment or condemnation, we showed each other love. No matter how dark the revelation, neither of us walked away.

Just like God does with us. He stands with us in our ugliness, in our darkness and continually holds out his hands to us — to guide us through, to haul us out. I am just amazed that he gave me another person to be his hands and heart in my life. — *Mary Elizabeth M.*

Notes

1. *Galaxy Quest*, directed by Dean Parisot, DreamWorks SKG, 1999.
2. William Shakespeare, *Macbeth*, 1.7.59-61.

CHAPTER 31

The Mother Network

Jack Byrnes: "Trust me, Greg, when you start having little Fockers running around, you'll feel the need for this type of security." From *Meet the Parents*[1]

My laugh has developed its own reputation, and perhaps by now, its own entry in Wikipedia. I have actually caused people to get up and move away from me in a movie theater. In my twenties, when I was doing costumes for theaters around Washington, D.C., people knew when I was in the audience. One night, an actor saw me after the show and said, "Hey, Melanie. I knew you were here tonight because I could hear you laughing from stage."

Sadly, over the years, my laugh has gotten worse with age, not better, and I've lost all ability to control it. You may be wondering what could cause such a horrible curse? That would be my mother. We look nothing alike. Our personalities are direct opposites. She majored in math; I majored in theatre. She's a bookkeeper; I'm a writer. She loves to bake with exact measurements; I love to experiment with whatever's on hand. She's blond; I'm brunette. She likes to stay home; I like to gad about the earth. Different.

The one thing we have in common is our laugh. It's a sucking, honking laugh. We suck-honk on different pitches, and my husband equates it to a couple of frolicking donkeys, "Eee-Ooh-Eee-Ooh."

Apparently this generational curse has nothing to do with genetics, because both my daughters, from two different continents and neither from my loins (Did I just say loins? Loins?!? None of my kids came from there. All my kids are loin-free.), have both started to imitate me. We are going to end up with a whole field of donkey frolickers.

Animalistic laughing aside, I'm developing one other commonality with my mother.

Mom Dating as Espionage

Growing up we'd joke about the Mother Network, how Mom got all her information, knew where we were at all times, perceived exactly what every kid in the neighborhood and at school was up to, and she'd have intimate knowledge of a situation before I'd even get home to tell her my version.

I know now that this was a result of intricate levels of mom dating with the "it-takes-a-village" model at its core. Mom dating as espionage. Safety of the kids comes first, with eyeballs in every window of every street in the neighborhood. They knew when I snuck into the woods to kiss a boy and they knew when my brother and his friends peed in the gulley.

As we got older and our world expanded, so did the Mother Network. Mom had the ability to mind meld with the moms of our friends who lived across town. They knew where we parked our cars and who had a drink at the cast party after the spring musical. (Not me, that's for sure. The Mother Network had me terrified that one drop would cause every brain cell to disintegrate on impact and I'd become a raging teenage alcoholic by morning. And the aspartame in Diet Coke would definitely destroy me. I stuck with strawberry Fanta, cuz nobody knew about red dye number 40 back then.)

> Mom had the ability to mind meld with the
> moms of our friends who lived across town.
> ===

The older my brother and I grew, the harder Mom prayed, and she joined a group of praying moms who met once a week to cover us all with their pleas to the Lord. They prayed for those of us who were falling away, falling down, and falling apart. They prayed for our friends, for our teachers, and they prayed for our school. These mamas developed a relationship with our school principal and prayed for her too. Some of us were broken and screwed up at the time, but I look back on that Mother Network and see how many of those prayers were answered.

> The older my brother and I grew,
> the harder Mom prayed . . .
> ===

My husband's mom has a Mother Network that has spanned decades and cross-country moves. She started raising her kids with a group of mamas when Alex and his sisters were tiny, and these ladies have stuck together. I've met them all, at weddings and on trips, and each woman in this network has continued to pray for and influence these grown-up children.

More Eyeballs

Now that I've survived my childhood and am developing my own Mother Network, I think about dating other moms so that like my mom, I have eyes and ears on my kids and we can help share the load of shepherding these littles through life. I also date other moms because having friends is fun.

Dating other moms will make you a better mom. You'll find accountability to take care of yourself and if you're married, your relationship with your spouse. You'll discover the sheer bliss of adult conversations, laughing till you snort, and your extreme joy will spill over onto your family. Your kids will see you model what it looks like to develop healthy relationships with peers. And your kids will have more eyeballs on them. It truly does take a village.

My son had a wonderful group of boys in his kindergarten class that he has remained friends with six years later. Their moms are still some of my closest friends today. As my son is getting older, playdates at the park where all the moms huddle up on the picnic table to compare stories about kids and life are getting fewer. Now we have to meet for breakfast or share weekly walks to keep up with our boys. I think there is an unspoken agreement between all of the moms. We are committed to making sure our boys stick together as they get older. Even though we love our mom time together it is just an added bonus. Getting to know each other over the years confirms that our boys belong together during those rocky teenage years. I feel so strongly that it is important to know the parents of my children's friends. I am truly thankful that the children and parents all enjoy each other. — Julie P.

Notes

1. *Meet the Parents*, directed by Jay Roach, Universal Pictures, 2000.

CHAPTER 32

What the World Needs Now

Joey: "It is a love based on giving and receiving as well as having and sharing. And the love that they give and have is shared and received. And through this having and giving and sharing and receiving, we too can share and love and have ... and receive."

From *Friends*[1]

"Just a mom." I've felt these words tumble out my mouth and plop on the toes of my brown leather boots like verbal bird poop.

What an asinine thing to say. There's no such thing as just a mom, and I'm going to be a little adamant about this.

I've said it. I say it over and over. And it's total crap. When we say we're "just" moms, we feed into a poisonous mentality that women aren't worth as much as men, and that motherhood isn't worth as much as other roles. When we say we're "just" moms, we also give ourselves an excuse not to rise into the full significance of what God can do through us.

This isn't about stay-at-home-work-from-home-work-out-of-the-home. Remember, we're all in this mom thing together. And this isn't about girl power or our need to create a sense of importance in our everyday lives.

It's about so much more. This is about God-power and the importance of aligning ourselves with our full potential in him. Mothers birth life, whether through our vaginas, our C-section gashes, or our reams of adoption paperwork. We nurture life, tending tears and coaxing giggles, teaching life's lessons and training up disciples. And we launch life, little ones into big ones and off into the wide world.

Mothers are the catalysts. Healing begins with us. So let's dream big. What if we could stop walking around wounded, share our burdens, and link arms around the world?

This call to dating moms isn't just something that I think is good. I think it's the way God designed us to live:

> And let us consider how we may spur one another on toward love and good deeds, not giving up meeting together, as some are in the habit of doing, but encouraging one another—and all the more as you see the Day approaching.   HEBREWS 10:24–25

I've spent a whole book writing about how I developed my momlationships. Now maybe I should take a little time to talk about why I bother.

It's About Me

I develop momlationships because it's fun. I love to laugh, and having friends in my life who remind me to laugh and give me something about which to laugh is positively joyous. Time flies when I'm partnering with other moms. While our kids play together, we parent together, and our days fill with ideas shared and dreams unleashed. Momlationships expand my myopic view of the bondage of the moment into a panorama of the journey together.

Over a cup of coffee or a large sweet tea, we celebrate everything that makes us who we are. We talk about motherhood, and we also discuss books, movies, likes and dislikes, our gentle opinions, and what we think about what's going on in the world. We are not just moms. We are never just moms. We are moms who have extraordinary ideas and can change the world as we change a diaper.

When I get out into the great big world with the mamas at my side and the kiddos at our feet, I recognize that I'm not just crawling toward a destination; this journey together is the destination, and I have arrived.

It's About My Family

My kids develop their own relationships with their peers as we regularly get together. We find a safe place in which to learn sharing and discipline. They discover that other families have boundaries too, and we learn about differences and how each family has its way of doing things, which leads to great conversations about identity as our individual family unit.

We fall in love with each other's kids as we fall in love with each other, and our kids experience a community of mamas who all cheer for them and rally around them. As I write these words, I'm around the world from two of my kids, and every day when I open up Facebook for a connection with my life back home, I'm blessed with messages from my friends who have seen my kids, checked up on them, and encouraged them during our time apart. I feel loved and cared for, and so do my littles.

> **Via Twitter @UnexpectedMel**
>
> In the school pickup line, I love watching that recognition as the kids see their parents. That bond, the I'm-with-you. Families are beautiful.

My mom has always said that friendships are hard work. To be a good friend, I think she is right. On the flip side anything worthwhile takes effort, and having girlfriends you can count on is priceless.

I feel so blessed to have friends in all the departments of my life. There are high school friends, college friends, friends of my children's friends, neighborhood friends, church friends, crafty friends, and exercise friends. I especially love when my girlfriends cross over into more than one department. It is comforting to have friends that want to share in all these parts of my life.

Once I had children I wanted them to learn how to be a good friend. I remember my husband and me searching for young couples with kids that could be our new amigos. I get really tongue-tied when meeting new people. So now that I have children, I usually let them lead the way. The majority of my time is spent with my children, so finding friendships where everyone has someone to play with is the best plan. — *Julie P.*

My marriage is stronger because of my momlationships, too. I did not see that one coming. When I was about to marry Alex, I feared losing the friendship with my college roommate. I worried that once I was married, I wouldn't need my girlfriend anymore, and I really loved her. I realize now how I never needed to worry about that, because I need my girlfriends now more than ever, and in fact, my girlfriends make me a better wife.

Via Twitter @UnexpectedMel

Hubby just said, "It would've been magic if Jane Austen had written comic books." Dude. Yes. This is why I love this man.

Alex and I have a wonderful marriage, but he can't relate to me as a woman. He understands me better than anyone, but he has a Y chromosome that keeps him from fully comprehending the way my mind works and the way I can think two hundred thoughts at one time while simultaneously experiencing three hundred different emotions. My mom dates take the pressure off him to provide all the empathy and advice I need to keep me calm enough to parent.

If it weren't for my momlationships, Alex wouldn't have friends, because I'm the one who scouts out everyone and then presents him with the appropriate bromantic opportunities. He needs my mom dating as much as I do.

It's About the World

What happens when we get ourselves and our relationships healthy? We become a minivan-driving force of nature. And I don't mean the way my van smells.

Some moms struggle with material poverty. Some moms struggle with relational poverty. When we relational-poverty mamas can work toward thriving momlationships, we unlock the potential to partner with our peers suffering from material poverty and make a difference in the lives of families around the world.

I live in suburban America, and we jokingly call our town "The Bubble." A little over four years ago, God took a gigantic needle and popped the bubble for me, and I became aware of a world on fire, millions in need of clean water, access to basic medical care, education, and food. Millions of men, women, and children enslaved and working to make the very goods that I consumed. Children dying of preventable diseases as I calmly dipped my nuggets in my favorite sauce and took my kids to the library for story time.

I felt like Neo from *The Matrix*. I'd taken the red pill and as the glossy digital world dissolved around me, I clawed my way out of my bubble and realized I'd been plugged into a machine. I could never go back.

At that point I went a little nuts. I started seeing everything as meals for children. That *grande* from Starbucks, that movie ticket, that shirt. I took a full year off of shopping for clothes, and I became an extremely intense person with whom to strike up a conversation. *Tell me more about sex trafficking, Melanie. We're also dying to hear more about the mosquito nets and malaria.*

After the bubble popped and I woke up to reality, God slowly led me to a new joy, and this joy contains all the pain of everything I've learned and seen with my own eyes and felt with my own hands. The children eating trash out of the dump. The victims of leprosy knitting scarves with no fingers. The girl with the gangrenous arm from a cook fire. The kids with distended bellies. The HIV-positive mother nursing her newborn baby. The village missing an entire generation due to war and disease.

God took all of that, all of it and more, opened my eyes to it, broke me into a million tiny pieces, then glued me back together with a joy forged in truth and hope. I know so much more than I knew before, and I know that together we can offer hope.

I couldn't handle any of it. I didn't want to know. But once I knew, I discovered this joy of partnering with other moms to make a difference. Now when I have a mom date, we share our frazzled tales of car pool capers and the nursing pad that fell out of a bra when someone bent over to sign her credit card slip, but we also might plan a fundraiser for the kids we sponsor or pray for an organization attempting to rescue a minor out of a brothel. Sometimes we encourage a friend who is fostering or adopting and give her a safe place to fall apart when things are hard.

I've seen a mom group date fund a meeting hall for orphans in Uganda, and I've seen moms sponsor other moms in Ethiopia so they could continue parenting the children they love. I've seen the prayers of mamas practically drop a kidney transplant from the sky, and a group of moms on Twitter raise enough money in a day to save a teen's life.

As we develop these momlationships that grow and shape our families, we get to create space for other mamas, for the ones around the world and the ones around the block, for the ones who are struggling. We need each other.

We aren't just moms. We are just a connected organism of nurturing world changers. And that is just awesome.

Bring out the snort laughing, movie quoting, and full-frontal hugging. Get out there, all you geeks and weirdos. The world is waiting, and you are fabulous.

Notes

1. "The One with the Vows," *Friends*, National Broadcasting Company, aired May 3, 2001.

Acknowledgments

I think I've used the word "newbie" at least a thousand times this year. I started prefacing emails with "newbie question," and the good people of Zondervan have never once made me feel like a moron as they guided me through the process of publishing.

Sandy Vander Zicht, it's a dream, an answer to ridiculous prayers I barely had the courage to mutter, to work with you. I stared at your business card for a couple of years and then schpedoinkle, there you were on the other end of the phone. Thanks for seeing something in my quirky writing and kicking group dates to second base where they belong.

Thank you, Alicia Kasen, for letting me have cannibalistic cake pops on the cover and for all your work getting the book into the hands of people who need to see cake pop cannibals. Thank you, Ben Greenhoe, for your work on the book trailer. You helped me run from a shark and cower from a Hydra. You're the best. Thank you, David Morris, Jennifer VerHage, Bridget Klein, Bridgette Brooks, and the rest of the Zondervan team. Seriously, I'm so honored to partner with you on this project.

Kathy Helmers, after our first phone call I told Alex you'd make me a better writer. You are encouraging and filled with integrity and wisdom. I'm so thankful for your experienced hands guiding me, and our texting banter is pretty much my favorite.

Jennifer Schuchmann, you open your mouth and wisdom and experience pour out, and I'm so grateful to you for taking my calls. Ever since you asked, "So, are you gonna tell me what your book is about?" my life hasn't been the same. Thanks for introducing me to Kathy.

To Logan Wolfram and the Allume team for creating the most nurturing and delightful place to find inspiration, thank you. You provided the doorway into this wonderful world and Allume feels like home.

To the readers of *Unexpected.org*, oh, you guys are gonna make me ugly cry. This book wouldn't be here without you. So this is all your fault. Thank you for the comments and community, for the likes and shares and follows and all the ways you guys took the original "Dating for Moms" post further than a tiny blogger could ever dream.

To the moms who sent in stories for the book, your perspectives made it better, richers, ours. Thank you for sharing your words.

As for my IRL mom friends, thanks for keeping me sane and for all the memories, the ones already made and the ones still to come. You aren't scary at all. Not even a little bit.

To my family, the one I grew up with and the one I married into, thanks for reading my blog when no one else did, and for traipsing along this unexpected life with me. Mom and Dad, thanks for feeding us and driving my kids around so I could squeeze in writing time.

Elliott, Evelyn, and Anastasia, you kids are my joy. Thanks for making me a mom, for helping me find friends, for your delightful shenanigans, and for all the times you let me pound away on my laptop. I love you SO BIG.

Alex, you're my best friend of all. You challenge and pull the very best out of me. Thanks for liking all the same movies and getting all the references. "Will you stop writing what I'm saying? Can we have one spontaneous conversation where my dialogue doesn't end up in your next story?"[1]

And Jesus, thanks for wrecking my life in all the best ways. I love you really, really a lot. Even though I don't understand everything, your Bible blows my mind and your grace rocks my face off.

Notes

1. *Kicking and Screaming*, directed by Noah Baumbach, Trimark Pictures, 1995.

Resources for Moms

Please be my friend and join me over at *Unexpected.org* to continue the conversation! I want to hear all about your mom-dating triumphs, your crash-and-burns, how you met your fourth-basers, dating horror stories, and all your scary and exhilarating tales of the mamas in your life. Let's laugh and learn from each other. Check out these organizations I mentioned in the book:

- Children's HopeChest—www.hopechest.org
- Sole Hope—www.solehope.org
- Sixty Feet—www.sixtyfeet.org
- Cupcake Kids—www.cupcakekids.org
- Ornaments for Orphans—www.ornaments4orphans.org
- Operation Christmas Child—
  www.operationchristmaschild.org
- AdoptUSKids—www.AdoptUSKids.org/
  join-the-conversation/ways-to-help

Here are some more mamas doing extraordinary things together:

- Forever We—www.ForeverWe.org. Nurtures the opportunity to live together with meaning and purpose, using dolls and books that represent the real issues kids are experiencing in the world today.
- Because Every Mother Matters—www.bemm.org. Strives to reduce the occurrences of maternal and infant mortality by providing sterile birthing kits, childbirth and development centers, education, and mother-to-mother sponsorships in Ethiopia.
- Project 143—www.p143.org. Emphasizes hosting older children, children with special needs, and sibling sets, as these kids are often the most forgotten or overlooked.

- Project Hopeful—www.ProjectHopeful.org. Brings hope to overlooked children and vulnerable mothers around the world.

If you and your mom friends get together and do something awesome for someone, I want to hear about it! Email me at womenarescary@unexpected.org.